IMPERIAL WAR
MUSEUM

THE SECOND WORLD WAR EXPERIENCE
TURNING OF THE TIDE

RICHARD OVERY

CARLTON

CONTENTS

ACKNOWLEDGEMENTS

I am happy to acknowledge the extent to which this book has been a real team effort. The book's editor Gemma Maclagan has played a key part in getting the book together and keeping me on schedule. Russell Knowles and Steve Behan are responsible for the book's strong visual content and layout. Philip Parker and Terry Charman have between them made sure that the history is as error-free as it can be and I am grateful to them for their scrupulous monitoring of the text and captions which has made this a better book.

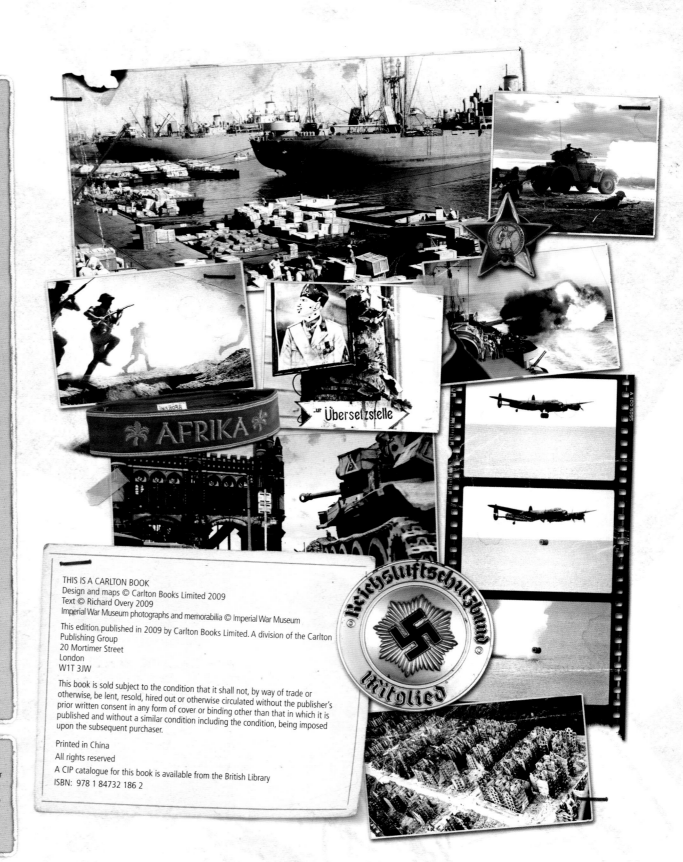

THIS IS A CARLTON BOOK
Design and maps © Carlton Books Limited 2009
Text © Richard Overy 2009
Imperial War Museum photographs and memorabilia © Imperial War Museum

This edition published in 2009 by Carlton Books Limited. A division of the Carlton Publishing Group
20 Mortimer Street
London
W1T 3JW

Printed in China
All rights reserved
A CIP catalogue for this book is available from the British Library
ISBN: 978 1 84732 186 2

INTRODUCTION

The Second World War was the largest and costliest war in human history. Its scale was genuinely global, leaving almost no part of the world unaffected. At its end the political geography of the world was transformed and the stage set for the emergence of the modern states' system. It is possible to exaggerate the break represented by victory in 1945, but the change between the prewar world of economic crisis, European imperialism and militant nationalism and the post-war world of economic boom, decolonisation and the ideological confrontation of the Cold War was a fundamental one.

It is worth remembering that no-one at the start could be certain what direction the war might take or could anticipate the degree of destruction and violence that it would draw in its wake. Different areas of conflict coalesced, like separate fires growing into a single inferno: the European conflict over German efforts to break the restrictions imposed after her defeat in World War I; the conflicts generated by an expansionist and ambitious Fascist Italy whose leader, Benito Mussolini, dreamed of recreating the Roman Empire; and the war for Asia fought by Imperial Japan, determined to assert the right of non-white peoples to a share of empire, and in central and eastern Europe by an alliance of anti-Communist states grouped around Hitler's Germany which launched a crusade against the Soviet system in 1941.

As the war grew in scope all the major powers were drawn in. It is often asserted that the entry of the United States in December 1941 made victory certain for the Allied powers through sheer economic weight, but the outcome was not preordained. Germany and her allies had large resources and captured yet more. German and Japanese forces fought with high skill. To win the war the Allies needed to improve fighting power, to co-ordinate their activities and to keep their populations, even in times of tribulation, committed to the cause. The idea that the Axis powers, and Germany in particular, lost the war through their own ineptitude distorts the extent to which the Allies had to learn to fight with greater effectiveness and to exploit their own scientific, technical and intelligence resources to the full. It is a measure of the significance they all gave to the war, not simply as the means to their own survival, but as a way to impose one world order or another, that they made the sacrifices they did. There was a powerful sense that this really was a war that would shape the way history would be made.

The Second World War Experience is the story of that conflict from its roots in the post-war settlement of 1919 to the final victory of the Allies and the re-establishment of a more stable world order. The fact that it is appearing in four volumes is testament to the huge scale and complexity of the wars fought in Europe, Asia, the Middle East and Africa and across the major oceans. The first two volumes covered the period of initial Axis aggression and the expansion of Axis territorial conquest to its fullest extent. The third volume covers that period of the war when the outcome was still in the balance in all the major theatres of conflict as the major Allies struggled desperately to halt the tide of advance. Slowly but surely on land and sea and in the air, the tide of war began to flow the Allies' way. It became clear that Axis forces, which had once seemed all but unstoppable, could be defeated in open battle. Victory in the desert war paved the way for the reconquest of the Mediterranean; victory in the Solomons opened a small doorway into the defensive frontier of the Japanese Empire through which the Allies poured overwhelming naval, air and military strength; victory at Stalingrad demonstrated to the world that the Red Army had come of age and the period of easy German victories was over. This volume ends with the Axis states pressed back on every front and the surrender of Mussolini's Italy, but some of the hardest and most costly battles of the climactic period of the war against Germany and Japan are the subject-matter of the final volume.

RICHARD OVERY, 2009

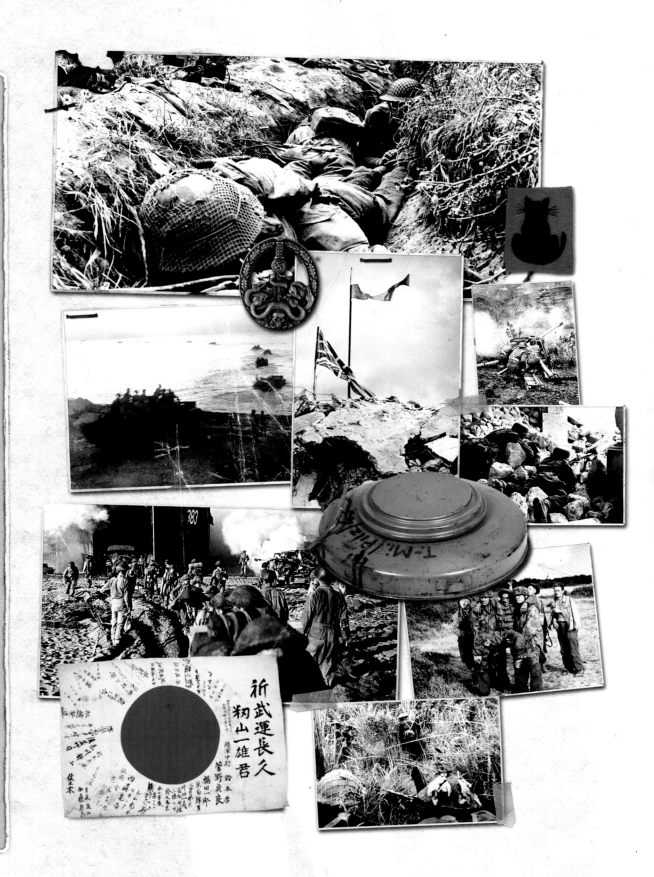

OPERATIONS 1942–1944

Battle of the North Cape:
the sinking of the Scharnhorst,
26–27 Dec. 1943

UNION OF SOVIET
SOCIALIST REPUBLICS

CANADA

GREAT
BRITAIN

GERMANY

FRANCE

ITALY

The Big Three:
The Teheran Conference,
28 Nov.–1 Dec. 1943

JAPAN

The Casablanca Conference:
"Unconditional Surrender",
14–24 Jan. 1943

Casablanca

Teheran

CHINA

UNITED STATES
OF AMERICA

INDIA

PACIFIC
OCEAN

ATLANTIC
OCEAN

FRENCH WEST
AFRICA

BRAZIL

INDIAN
OCEAN

see right

see bottom right

AUSTRALIA

SOUTH
AFRICA

GENERAL MAP KEY — TO SPREAD MAPS

military units

XXXXX	Army Group
XXXX	Army
XXX	Corps
XX	Division
X	Brigade
III	Regiment
II	Battalion
I	Company

military types

	Infantry
	Armour
	Airborne
	Mechanised

nationalities

	German		French
	Italian		Romanian
	Japanese		Finnish
	United States		Vichy (named)
	British		Hungarian
	Soviet		other (named)

EUROPE MAP KEY

	AXIS STATE, 1943
	AXIS ALLIED STATES, 1943
	AXIS OCCUPIED, 1943
	LIMIT OF AXIS EXPANSION EASTWARDS, 1942

FAR EAST MAP KEY

	JAPANESE EMPIRE, 1943
	JAPANESE ALLIED STATES
	LIMIT OF JAPANESE EXPANSION, 1942

ABOVE & RIGHT

The years 1942–1944 were the turning point of the war. In 1942 Japanese advances into south-east Asia, Burma and the Pacific islands created a large new area of Japanese imperial rule. In Germany, following a slowdown of the German attack in the winter of 1941–2, a renewed campaign in southern Russia brought German forces to the Volga and the Caucasus mountains. In North Africa by mid-1942 Axis forces were deep in Egyptian territory. From this point on the Allies began to organise an effective defence and then begin a slow programme of offensives in the Pacific islands, in the North African desert and deep inside Soviet territory which pushed the Axis forces back. Italy was invaded in 1943 and surrendered in September of that year, and the Red Army reached into the Ukraine by the end of 1943. By the middle of 1944 the stage was set for the final desperate struggle for Europe and the Far East.

IRELAND

Dublin

Cork

Rationing:
the War for Food

Plymouth

Atlantic
Ocean

Engli

Cherbourg

Brest

The French Resistance

Nan

F

Borde

Bilbao

Toulous

PORTUGAL

Tagus

Madrid

Barcelo

Douro

Ebro

SPAIN

Balearic

Gibraltar
(British)

SPAINISH MOROCCO

Oran

Alg

Operation "Torch",
8 Nov.–Feb. 1943

MOROCCO

AL

AFRICA

SWEDEN

North
Sea

DENMARK

• Copenhagen

**The Bombing of Hamburg:
Operation "Gomorrah",
24–25 Jul. 1943**

• Hamburg

Baltic
Sea

Riga

LATVIA

LITHUANIA

Dvina

• Dünaburg

Wilna •

REICHSKOMMISSARIAT
OSTLAND

• Smolensk

SOVIET

• Vladimir

• Moscow

• Riga

Tula •

• Ryazan

UNION

• Orel

• Tambov

TED
DOM

erpool
anchester

• Birmingham

• London

rtsmouth
annel

**The Secret War:
spies, codes and
deception**

NETHERLANDS

• Amsterdam
• Rotterdam

BELGIUM

• Brussels
• Lille

Caen •

• Paris

Seine

NCE

• Bremen

• Hanover

• Berlin

Elbe

GERMAN EMPIRE

Danzig •

East
Prussia

Königsberg •

Vistula

Stettin •

**Dambusters,
7 May 1943**

LUXEMBOURG

• Frankfurt

Rhine

• Leipzig

Oder

Lodz •

Partisan War

• Warsaw

• Brest

GENERAL
GOVERNMENT

• Minsk

Mogilev •

• Gomel

• Briansk

REICHSKOMMISSARIAT

UKRAINE

Kiev •

Dnieper

Dnieper

Don

• Kharkov

• Kursk

**The Battle of Kursk,
5–13 Jul. 1943**

**From Kharkov to Kiev:
the Red Army Breaks Through,
23 Aug. – 6 Nov. 1943**

**Defeat at Stalingrad,
19 Nov. – 2 Feb. 1943**

**The Battle for Stalingrad,
19 Aug.–19 Nov. 1942**

• Stalingrad

Volga

**The Soviet Counter-Stroke:
Operation "Uranus",
19 Nov. – 24 Dec. 1942**

• Metz

Lyons •

• Strassburg

Stuttgart •

SWITZERLAND

Loire

Rhône

Marseille •

• Turin

Genoa •

Corsica

Sardinia

• Cagliari

**Anzio, 22 Jan.–
24 May 1944**

• Prague

BOHEMIA

• Munich

AUSTRIA

Danube

• Vienna

SLOVAKIA

• Cracow

Lemberg •

Dniester

• Budapest

HUNGARY

• Debrecen

• Timisoara

ROMANIA

CROATIA

Po

• Trieste

ITALY

Rome •

Anzio •

**The Battle for
Monte Cassino,
17 Jan.–9 May 1943**

• Naples

• Salerno

• Taranto

Nikolayev •

• Kherson

• Odessa

Chisinau •

Black
Sea

Perekop •

CRIMEA

Sea of
Azov

• Kerch

Sevastopol •

Taganrog •

• Rostov-on-Don

• Novorossiisk

ITALIA

**Italy: Invasion and Surrender,
3–8 Sep. 1943**

Palermo •

Messina •

**Operation "Husky":
the Capture of Sicily,
9 Jul.–17 Aug. 1943**

Tunis •

**The End of the Axis
in Africa: Tunisia,
19 Feb.–13 May
1943**

TUNISIA

• Mareth

Malta
(British)

Mediterranean
Sea

RIA

• Tripoli

LIBYA

• El Agheila

• Benghazi

Dera •

**Second Alamein,
23 Oct.–4 Nov. 1942**

**The Tide Turns in North Africa:
Alam Halfa, 13–30 Aug. 1942**

• El Alamein

• Alexandria

Suez Canal

EGYPT

Nile

PALESTINE

TRANSJORDAN

MONGOLIA

MANCHURIA

CHINA

**Operation "Longshot":
the Chindits in Burma,
8 Feb.–30 Apr. 1943**

INDIA

**Battle for India:
Imphal,
8 May–3 Jul.;
Kohima,
4 Apr.–22 Jun. 1944**

• Rangoon

BURMA

SIAM

Ceylon

FRENCH
INDO-
CHINA

• Saigon

MALAY STATES

• Singapore

Borneo

Jakata •

Celebes

DUTCH EAST INDIES

Timor

INDIAN OCEAN

• Nanking

Shanghai •

Kunming •

• Hong Kong

KOREA

• Tokyo

Formosa

**Japan's War in China:
Operation "Ichi-Go",
18 April–Nov. 1944**

• Manila

PHILIPPINES

JAPAN

PACIFIC
OCEAN

Iwo Jima

Mariana
Islands

Saipan

Guam

Truk

Midway

Hawaiian
Islands

Wake Island

Marshall
Islands

**Island-Hopping in the Pacific:
The Gilbert and Marshall
Islands, 20 Nov.–17 Feb. 1944**

Gilbert
Islands

**Operation "Cartwheel":
the war for New Guinea,
30 Jun.–Mar. 1944**

Hollandia

New Guinea

• Rabaul

Solomon
Islands

Port Moresby •

AUSTRALIA

**Guadalcanal,
12 Nov. 1942–8 Feb. 1943**

05

THE TIDE TURNS IN NORTH AFRICA

When Rommel's successful Axis offensive reached into Egypt to the Alamein Line in June 1942, he was determined to push on to capture Cairo and the Suez Canal. His success in the summer offensive had earned him the rank of field marshal. On 1 July, the Axis forces attacked the Allied defensive line but British Commonwealth forces were dug in well and the attacks were repulsed. General Auchinleck then decided on a counter-offensive, taking advantage of a substantial superiority in tanks and aircraft. The attacks, launched on 10 July, proved a costly failure. Rommel was prevented from going any further, but Allied tank strength, which had been four times that of Rommel's forces, was severely reduced. Allied casualties from what became known as the First Battle of El Alamein were over 13,000.

Churchill, frustrated at repeated failure, removed Auchinleck and replaced him as commander-in-chief Middle East with General Harold Alexander. Command of the 8th Army was given to Lieutenant General William Gott, but he died on 7 August, when the transport plane in which he was travelling was shot down. His replacement, Lieutenant General Bernard Montgomery, was to forge a remarkable alliance with Alexander which led Allied armies across North Africa and on into Sicily and Italy. Montgomery was reluctant to commit to a further offensive until he had substantial additional forces; instead the defensive line was strengthened in anticipation of a further German assault, whose details had been revealed by ULTRA decrypts.

Rommel's plan was to mount a diversionary attack towards the Australian and South African forces on the coast around El Alamein, while taking the bulk of his armour and that of his Italian ally in a wide southern sweep to outflank the Allied line and encircle Montgomery's forces.

ABOVE Italian Fascism continued to pretend that Italy was a powerful military state despite defeats in Africa. Here a wartime military parade in front of visiting German dignitaries in the Piazza Venezia in Rome is supposed to display the might of the new Italy.

FIELD MARSHAL HAROLD ALEXANDER (1891–1969)

Harold Alexander was one of Britain's most successful wartime commanders. After a distinguished combat career in the First World War, he became the youngest general in the army in 1937. He commanded the First Division in France in 1940 and then commanded the BEF (British Expeditionary Force) during the Dunkirk evacuation. In March 1942 he organized the British retreat from Burma, and was appointed commander-in-chief Middle East in August 1942. In early 1943 he became Eisenhower's deputy for the campaign in Tunisia, where he reorganized a poorly co-ordinated Allied front and forced Axis surrender in May. He commanded the invasion of Sicily and Italy and in November 1944 was made supreme commander in the Mediterranean. Created a field marshal in September 1944, he was governor general of Canada from 1946 to 1952.

ABOVE A German soldier uses a "donkey's ears" periscope to observe Allied lines during the probing attacks organized by Rommel in early July 1942.

OBJECT Armband awarded to German forces who took part in the North Africa campaigns.

It was an ambitious but predictable move and Montgomery prepared his forces to meet the encircling Axis on the high ridge at Alam Halfa, some 25 kilometres (15 miles) behind Allied lines. Short of fuel and with a limited number of tanks, Rommel began the attack on the night of 30/31 August with four armoured units, the German 15th and 21st Panzer, and the Italian Ariete and Littorio divisions. They made rapid progress through the series of defensive

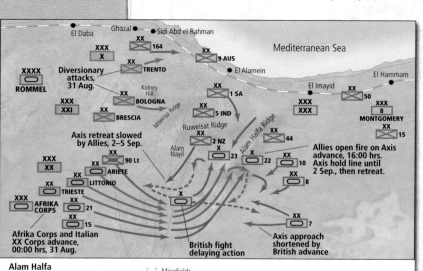

El Daba Ghazal Sidi Abd el Rahman

Mediterranean Sea

XXX X 164

XXXX ROMMEL Diversionary attacks, 31 Aug. XX TRENTO XX 9 AUS

XXX XXI Kidney Hill XX BOLOGNA El Alamein

XX BRESCIA XX 1 SA El Imayid

Mharib Ridge XX 5 IND XXX XXX El Hammam

Ruweisat Ridge XXX XXX XXX 8 MONTGOMERY

Axis retreat slowed by Allies, 2–5 Sep. XX 2 NZ X XX 23 X Alam Halfa Ridge XX 22 XX 10 XX 15

XXX XX XX 90 Lt Alam Nayil XX 44 Allies open fire on Axis advance, 16:00 hrs. Axis hold line until 2 Sep., then retreat.

XX ARIETE XX 8

XX LITTORIO

XXX AFRIKA CORPS XX 21

XX 15 XX 7

Afrika Corps and Italian XX Corps advance, 00:00 hrs, 31 Aug. British fight delaying action Axis approach shortened by British advance

Alam Halfa 31 August–5 September 1942   ⚡ Minefields

"boxes" on the south of the Allied line and turned on Alam Halfa ridge to complete the encirclement.

Montgomery's strategy worked just as intended. Axis forces became bogged down in extensive minefields, were attacked on the flank by the British 7th Armoured Division and hit by effective anti-tank fire from forces dug in on the ridge. After two days of fruitless fighting, Rommel ordered a retreat, leaving 50 tanks and 400 vehicles behind. This was the furthest Axis forces got in the North African campaign, and the last prospect that Rommel had of snatching a rapid victory. Over the next two months Rommel established a thick defensive line against the expected counter-offensive, with wide minefields and armoured divisions dug in behind them.

The victory at Alam Halfa has attracted none of the attention given to the eventual victory at Alamein in November, but it was an important turning point and it gave Montgomery the opportunity to display his mettle while Churchill pressed him for action. It was a victory won by substantial superiority in weapons and supplies. The Middle Eastern air force comprised 96 squadrons of more than 1,000 aircraft by October 1942, with a genuinely international flavour. Beside units staffed by British crew, there were American, South African, Australian, Greek, Canadian, French, Rhodesian and Yugoslav squadrons. Air power proved a substantial bonus for Allied forces as the German and Italian air component dwindled, hampered by regular shortages of fuel oil. These advantages were to prove decisive in the next, and most famous, of Montgomery's offensives.

ABOVE British forces depended on generous supplies from the United States for the Middle Eastern campaigns. Here the 5th Royal Tank Regiment displays its Grant tanks for the camera on 17 February 1942.

BELOW Supply was a big advantage the Allies held over the Axis in North Africa because Axis supply routes were easily interrupted by Allied submarine and air attack. Here a convoy unloads RAF parts and equipment in Port Said in Egypt in August 1942.

ABOVE Churchill flew to Cairo in August 1942 to see for himself what should be done to ensure that North Africa could be defended. Here he sits with the South African premier Jan Smuts with, behind, General Alan Brooke (right) and Air Marshal Arthur Tedder (left).

THE BATTLE FOR STALINGRAD

26 AUGUST 1942
General Zhukov appointed deputy supreme commander-in-chief under Stalin.

12 SEPTEMBER 1942
British liner *Laconia* sunk in the South Atlantic with 1,500 Italian POWs on board.

3 OCTOBER 1942
German rocket scientists successfully launch the A4 missile which was to become the V2 rocket.

18 OCTOBER 1942
Hitler orders that all British commandos who fall into German hands are executed.

4 NOVEMBER 1942
Axis forces in Egypt under Rommel are forced to retreat after defeat in the Second Battle of Alamein.

8 NOVEMBER 1942
Allied forces land in northwest Africa in Operation "Torch".

11 NOVEMBER 1942
German forces occupy Vichy France in reaction to the Allied landings in North Africa.

ABOVE German artillerymen give close support to the infantry as they edge forward through the ruins of Stalingrad. The picture is from November 1942, shortly before the encirclement of the 6th Army.

GENERAL VASILY CHUIKOV (1900–82)
Chuikov was the son of a peasant family who joined the Red Army during the Russian Civil War. He became a career officer and in 1939 commanded the Soviet 4th Army in the occupation of Poland. His poor performance in the Soviet-Finnish war led to his demotion and he was sent as adviser to Chiang Kaishek in China. He was recalled in May 1942 and posted a few weeks later to command the 64th Army trying to hold the steppe in front of Stalingrad. In September he was transferred to command of the 62nd Army in the defence of the city itself, and distinguished himself as an inspiring, brave and innovative commander. He later commanded the army that reached the centre of Berlin first, in May 1945. In 1955, he was promoted to marshal and was commander-in-chief of the Soviet army from 1960 to 1964. He was buried in Stalingrad on the hill of Mamayev Kurgan, scene of the most bitter fighting in the city.

When German and Romanian forces finally reached the outskirts of Stalingrad in mid-August and forced a small salient as far as the Volga river in the north, there was wide confidence at Hitler's headquarters that the city would be in German hands in a matter of days; weeks at the most. On 19 August, Paulus launched a major offensive against the city together with some units of the 4th Panzer Army. On 23 August, the German air force in southern Russia, commanded by General (later Field Marshal) Wolfram von Richthofen, sent 600 bombers to devastate the city. The decision to leave the population in place to avoid the disruption that would be caused by a stream of refugees resulted, according to Soviet estimates, in the death of 40,000 people. The savage bombardment from artillery and aircraft pushed the Soviet defenders back towards the river.

On 7 September, Paulus massed his forces for a concerted push to drive the Soviet defenders across the Volga. The two armies defending the area, 62nd and 64th, were split apart and block by block, factory by factory, German forces pressed forward. The commander of the 62nd, General Lopatin, thought the situation was hopeless and argued for withdrawal. He was dismissed and his place taken by a young, ebullient commander, Vasily Chuikov. He arrived the same day as the German thrust on 7 September to find a city in ruins. The Red Army survived only by using the destroyed urban landscape as a natural defence. In cellars and warehouses small groups of soldiers hid themselves, sniping at German infiltrators, using the cover of night to retake buildings that had been abandoned to heavier German daytime firepower. During September and October, the German army pushed the 62nd back into a handful of factory complexes – the Red October factory, the Barricades

ABOVE German soldiers storm part of the Red October plant near the edge of the Volga River in the heart of Stalingrad. Each building was fought for room by room.

BELOW Under "rolling cover" from storm artillery forces, German infantry enter the suburbs of Stalingrad, 12 November 1942.

ABOVE Soviet troops stage a counter-attack on German forces in the vicinity of the Red October plant, 26 November 1942.

factory – right on the edge of the river.

Neither Paulus nor Chuikov fought a campaign entirely isolated from the rest of the Axis and Soviet forces. A stream of supplies and reinforcements crossed the Volga from the far bank; artillery and rocket fire was directed at German strongholds from the same area. On either flank of the city were much larger Soviet armies: to the south General Yeremenko's Stalingrad Army Group, to the north the Don Army Group of General Rokossovsky. They provided what assistance they could by attacking the exposed flanks of the German armies, while overhead large numbers of Soviet aircraft, directed in a co-ordinated way by radio (the earliest example of this), began to contest local air superiority for almost the first time in the campaign. German forces were stretched out across the Don Steppe, with the vulnerable corridor into Stalingrad guarded by Hungarian, Italian and Romanian allies. The German 4th Air Fleet was pressed heavily by the battle, but continued to provide assistance to

FIELD MARSHAL FRIEDRICH PAULUS (1890–1957)

Friedrich Paulus was unusual among top German officers in coming from a bourgeois background, though he is often mistakenly described as "von Paulus". The son of a schoolmaster, he served in the German army continuously from 1910. In the 1930s his reputation as a very effective staff officer brought him rapid promotion. By 1939 he was chief-of-staff of the German 10th Army, which was renamed 6th Army for the campaign in Belgium and France. He played a major part in preparing the staff plans for Operation "Barbarossa", and took over command of the 6th Army in January 1942 following the sudden death of Field Marshal Walter von Reichenau. He was captured at Stalingrad and became a major figure in the Soviet-sponsored National Committee Free Germany, made up of German POWs. After the war he returned to East Germany, where he worked as an inspector of police.

the ground war as well as challenging Soviet air power.

The determination of the 62nd Army to hold the city at all costs has sometimes been attributed to fear of Soviet security forces in the rear who would shoot deserters or defeatists, or send them off to penal battalions. A figure of 13,500 has been estimated for those shot by their own side. But Soviet records show only 203 arrests for "panic" from November 1942 to February 1943 among all the Soviet armies defending Stalingrad. The evidence from eye-witnesses suggests instead that the Soviet defenders had at last found a cause they could

ОТСТОИМ ВОЛГУ-МАТУШКУ!

ABOVE Propaganda played an important part in keeping the Red Army fighting at Stalingrad. Vladimir Serov's 1942 poster reads "Let's Defend the Volga!".

OBJECT Medal awarded to Soviet troops for "success in combat".

LEFT Almost all of Stalingrad was destroyed during the bombing and shelling of the city. Residents continued to eke out a living where they could in cellars and ruins, but at least 40,000 civilians died in the battle.

identify with and a military challenge that made sense. The Russian novelist Viktor Nekrasov, who served as a junior officer at Stalingrad, found that the battle produced "wonderfully hardened soldiers". German soldiers also fought with great tenacity and desperation. The urban battlefield became a small, enclosed, violent microcosm of the larger battle that surrounded it.

On 9 November, German forces finally succeeded in punching a 500-metre (550-yard) hole in Chuikov's front, reaching the Volga. Soviet troops could not dislodge them, but German exhaustion brought a lull on 12 November. Six days later, Chuikov received a cryptic message from front headquarters that he should stand by for special orders. On the morning of 19 November, Chuikov was told that a massive Soviet counter-offensive had just been launched whose purpose was to cut off and encircle Paulus's 6th Army.

SECOND ALAMEIN

The Second Battle of El Alamein was the first major victory of British Commonwealth forces against the German enemy and it opened the way to the destruction of Axis forces throughout North Africa. Although the battle was dwarfed by the campaigns on the Eastern Front, it was nonetheless a decisive turning point in Allied fortunes, making the Middle East secure and opening the way for a campaign to liberate the Mediterranean from the Axis.

Rommel knew after the failure at Alam Halfa that he lacked the depth of resources needed to penetrate further into Egypt. Instead, he established a thick defensive line, providing German troops and tanks to strengthen the Italian divisions; the greatest concentration of Axis forces was in the north, protecting communications along the coast. Rommel had four German and a maximum of eight Italian divisions at his disposal (a balance reflected in the decision to rename Panzer Army Africa the German-Italian Panzer Army). The Axis fielded around 500 tanks, of which fewer than half were German, and had support from 350

13 AUGUST 1942
Montgomery takes over as commander of the 8th Army.

14 OCTOBER 1942
German forces begin major assault on Stalingrad defences to drive Red Army into the Volga.

31 OCTOBER 1942
Heavy German bombing raid on the English cathedral city of Canterbury.

ABOVE Formation badge for the British 7th Armoured Division, known as the "Desert Rats".

ABOVE Badge of the 51st Highland Infantry Division.

LEFT British infantry advance through the dust and smoke of combat during the Second Battle of Alamein, October 1942.

ABOVE Italian soldiers on the Egyptian front at El Alamein in action against Allied forces. Some 60 per cent of the Axis troops at Alamein were Italian.

aircraft. All Axis forces were short of fuel and spare parts. Montgomery, on the other hand, saw his forces grow steadily during September and October. The armoured divisions could call on 1,030 tanks, 300 of which were new American Grants, and there were over 1,500 aircraft in the Middle East and Malta. He refused to act until he was confident that his forces had a decisive superiority and the army understood the nature of his plan.

After years of rapid mobile warfare, the Second Alamein battle was a set-piece operation. Montgomery planned to attack where Rommel was strongest in the north, around Kidney Hill, but to disguise the weight of his assault by diversionary attacks in the south. His object, in what was codenamed Operation "Lightfoot", was to send forward the infantry divisions to open up a pathway through the minefields, and then to pour the tanks of the 10th Armoured Corps through the gap. With a salient secured, a second operation, "Supercharge", would push through large armoured forces for the final blow. The start was set for 23 October, when fortuitously Rommel was away on sick leave.

BELOW German soldiers man the tank-busting 88-millimetre (3.5-inch) anti-aircraft gun during the Battle of Alamein. It was found that the gun could be used against tanks as well as aircraft and was very effective against Allied tanks throughout the war.

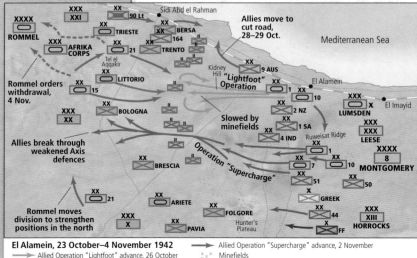

Allies move to cut road, 28–29 Oct.

Mediterranean Sea

Sidi Abd el Rahman

ROMMEL

AFRIKA CORPS

Rommel orders withdrawal, 4 Nov.

Allies break through weakened Axis defences

Tel el Aqqakir

Kidney Hill "Lightfoot" Operation

El Alamein

Slowed by minefields

Ruweisat Ridge

El Imayid

LUMSDEN

LEESE

Operation "Supercharge"

MONTGOMERY

Rommel moves division to strengthen positions in the north

Hunter's Plateau

GREEK

HORROCKS

El Alamein, 23 October–4 November 1942
→ Allied Operation "Lightfoot" advance, 26 October
→ Allied Operation "Supercharge" advance, 2 November
✕ Minefields

FIELD MARSHAL BERNARD MONTGOMERY (1887–1976)

The son of an Anglo-Irish clergyman, Montgomery joined the army in 1908 and saw service in the early battles of the First World War before a bullet in the lung almost killed him. He returned to duty as a staff officer, and served between the wars in Ireland, India, Egypt and Palestine, where he was responsible for suppressing a revolt in 1938. He made his reputation as an excellent trainer of men and a master of meticulous preparation. In the Battle of France he commanded the 3rd Division, which he successfully withdrew at Dunkirk with relatively low casualties. In December 1941 he was appointed commander-in-chief Southeastern Command, where he insisted on intensive training for his men. Appointed to command the 8th Army in August 1942, he transformed its morale in a matter of weeks. El Alamein was his most famous victory, and subsequent campaigns in Sicily, Italy and northwest Europe made him a household name. He was a difficult personality – acerbic, intolerant, boastful, egotistical – and this soured his strategic performance. He collaborated poorly with others; tact was entirely foreign to him. He was ground commander for the Normandy invasion, then commander of the 21st Army Group. After the war, he was appointed chief of the Imperial General Staff and created Viscount Montgomery of Alamein.

ENCLOSURES

1. Diary of Bombardier Leslie Coleman of the 14th Light Anti-Aircraft Regiment, New Zealand Expeditionary Force, 25 October to 12 November 1942. The entries cover the key period of the Second Battle of Alamein and the long Axis retreat.

2. Diary of Corporal Herbert Jesse, a soldier in Rommel's Panzergruppe Afrika, from 18 October to 14 November 1942, covering the period of the Second Battle of Alamein and the subsequent retreat of German forces. Jesse records the heavy British artillery bombardments and air attacks that signalled the start of the battle.

3. Orders of General Bernard Montgomery for the third day of the Second Battle of Alamein, 26 October 1942, codenamed Operation "Lightfoot". Fierce German counter-attacks were met by regrouping British Commonwealth forces. A week later the Axis line was broken and Rommel in retreat.

Operation "Lightfoot" began with a massive artillery barrage in the evening of 23 October. Rommel's replacement, Lieutenant General Stumme, died during the Allied air attacks, leaving Axis forces in some confusion until Rommel's return on 25 October. Nevertheless, resistance was fierce, and only by the second day was progress made along the coast road and around Kidney Hill. Rommel ordered his tanks north to dislodge the enemy, but exposed the Italian divisions to Allied attacks, which were pressed forward during fierce armoured fighting on 27 and 28 October. Montgomery then withdrew the diversionary forces in the south and concentrated a heavy armoured force to carry out "Supercharge". When the fresh armour poured through on 2 November, supported by strong air attacks, Rommel realized he was defeated; Axis forces were down to only 35 fully serviceable tanks. Hitler refused permission to withdraw, but two days later he had to accept reality, and Rommel began a rapid westwards retreat along the coast road. Some Italian divisions continued to fight after the German forces had abandoned the battle, but the Axis position was hopeless. Rommel left over 400 destroyed tanks; the Allies lost around 250. Allied casualties were 13,500, but Montgomery's forces netted over 30,000 Axis prisoners.

The 8th Army raced in pursuit of the retreating Rommel and by 13 November had retaken Tobruk. Axis forces made brief defensive attacks at Benghazi on 20 November and El Agheila between 23 November and 13 December, but the pressure was relentless. Tripoli was occupied on 23 January and Rommel raced for the last defensive line in Tunisia, the Mareth Line, where Axis forces finally halted and turned. Victory at Alamein was complete and permission was given for church bells in Britain to ring out in celebration for the first time since May 1940.

ABOVE Sherman tanks of the Allied armoured forces in North Africa move swiftly along desert routes in pursuit of the retreating German and Italian forces after the victory at El Alamein in November 1942.

RIGHT A British Daimler-Benz armoured car opens fire at the start of the attack on German-held Tripoli, 18 January 1943. The port fell to the Allies five days later.

BELOW A British Bofors mobile anti-aircraft gun being moved forward in November 1942 to the Libyan frontier, past a dead German soldier, left unburied during the rapid Axis retreat.

MARSHAL UGO CAVALLERO (1880–1943)

A member of the Piedmontese nobility, Cavallero joined the Italian army in 1898 and rose rapidly on account of his organizational and tactical skills. He fought in the Italo-Turkish war of September 1911–October 1912, and during the First World War joined the Italian Supreme Command where he rose to be chief of operations responsible for organizing the Italian victory at Vittorio Veneto. He was a keen Fascist and served as undersecretary of war during 1925–28. He left the army but was recalled in 1937 and took command of Italian forces in East Africa the following year. In December 1940, he succeeded Badoglio as chief of the Italian Supreme Command, and took personal control of the Italian forces in Greece, where he stabilized the front line. He was nominally Rommel's superior for the Axis campaigns in North Africa, but found it difficult to overrule his German allies. He opposed Rommel's invasion of Egypt, and when Libya was lost following Alamein, he was sacked. He committed suicide in September 1943 after refusing Hitler's request to lead those Italian forces still committed to fighting the Allies.

OPERATION "TORCH"

BELOW The "white ensign" hoisted by a British naval signal party after landing west of Algiers in the early hours of 8 November 1942 as part of Operation "Torch".

In the summer of 1942 the British and American chiefs-of-staff discussed the possibility of opening a "second front" in France in 1942. A frontal assault was rejected as too risky with unproven American forces and shortages of shipping, and on 22 July it was agreed to launch a smaller combined-arms assault on French North Africa. The object was to help the British in the east to clear the Axis out of Libya and to give American forces an opportunity to gain combat experience. The operation, codenamed "Torch", was to be largely an American affair and it was placed under the command of the recently arrived Lieutenant General Eisenhower.

The plan was to land substantial forces in French Morocco, and at Oran and Algiers in Algeria. It was hoped that the large French garrisons could be persuaded not to oppose the landings, and on 22 October Eisenhower's deputy, Major General Mark Clark, landed secretly in Algeria to make contact with the local commander of French forces, but a guarantee could not be secured that there would be

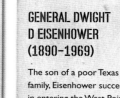

no resistance. The task force sailed in two large formations. The men and equipment for the Moroccan landings under Major General George Patton sailed directly across the Atlantic. A vast armada of 650 warships took the forces for the central and eastern sectors from British ports. The total assault force of 65,000 men was roughly half the size of the French garrison, but was strongly supported by naval vessels and by two large air forces, one for the western landings, one for the east.

The landings on 8 November achieved complete surprise since the fleet was disguised as a convoy bound for Malta. There was strong resistance in Morocco and also in Oran, but in Algiers the situation was confused by a coup launched by 400 French resistance fighters on the day of the

ABOVE LEFT Grumman Wildcat fighters and Supermarine Seafires, the naval version of the Spitfire, wait to take off from the flightdeck of HMS *Formidable* in support of the landings in Operation "Torch", November 1942.

LEFT American troops of the Centre Task Force aboard a landing craft on their way towards the beaches near the Algerian port of Oran.

BELOW Troops landing on the beach at Arzeu near Oran on the morning of 8 November 1942, prelude to two days of fighting before the city surrendered.

ABOVE A US officer talking to Algerians shortly after the "Torch" landings.

BELOW RIGHT The German occupation of Vichy France on 11 November 1942 followed the successful "Torch" landings. Here German tanks enter Toulouse in southwestern France.

RIGHT A Moroccan sergeant major of the French North African Army pictured on the cover of Picture Post, 28 November 1942. Moroccan and Algerian units joined the Free French at once and were used in the subsequent invasion of Italy.

PICTURE POST

A NEW ARMY FOR THE ALLIES
A Sergeant-Major of the French North-African Army.
(See pages 13 to 17)

HULTON'S NATIONAL WEEKLY

In this issue: ITALY'S CHOICE 4D
by TOM WINTRINGHAM
NOVEMBER 28, 1942 Vol. 17. No. 9

landings which immobilized some of the troops and brought the occupation of most government buildings. Vichy forces fought back and tried to resist the Allied landing, but Admiral Darlan, overall commander-in-chief of Vichy French forces, who happened to be in Algiers, finally agreed to a ceasefire, but then promptly tried to withdraw it when the Vichy government refused to endorse his decision. Arrested by the American authorities, he agreed on 10 November to order a ceasefire in Oran, and the following day gave orders for an end to hostilities in Morocco.

The response to the Allied landings was immediate: on 10 November, Hitler ordered the German occupation of Vichy-controlled France; Italian forces occupied Corsica; and Vichy was compelled to agree to the transfer of Axis forces in large numbers to the as yet unoccupied French territory of Tunisia. Darlan tried to persuade the French fleet to sail to North Africa and join the Allies, but the naval command refused and on 27 November the fleet was scuttled at Toulon. When Darlan was murdered on 24 December, his place was taken by the pro-Allied General Giraud and French forces willing to fight with the Allies were placed under the field command of General Juin.

The landings were supposed to clear the way to link up with Montgomery's now advancing 8th Army in Libya, but in the race to reach Tunisia the German and Italian forces acted faster, bringing 17,000 troops and substantial numbers of aircraft into the area around Tunis by the end of November.

In the south, Rommel reached the defensive Mareth Line and almost the whole of Tunisia was in Axis hands. A combined British and American 1st Army tried to reach Tunis and came within 20 kilometres (32 miles) of their target, but the newly created 5th Panzer Army under General von Arnim succeeded in preventing the breakthrough and the 1st Army ground to a halt in poor weather and deep mud. During January 1943, the Axis forces succeeded in a number of small operations in pushing back French and British forces and stabilizing a defensive line in the Dorsale Mountains. By early February, with Rommel's forces arrived in Tunisia, a formidable garrison had been formed. An operation that had promised a quick end to the Axis presence in North Africa had instead provoked a final stand.

ENCLOSURE
Planning report drawn up in September 1942 by Major General Patton for Lieutenant General Eisenhower, overall commander of the Allied forces for the North African landings. Patton was responsible for the American Western Task Force in Operation "Torch", which landed on the coast of Morocco around Casablanca on 8 November 1942.

ADMIRAL FRANÇOIS DARLAN (1881–1942)

Darlan was a successful and ambitious French naval officer, who joined the navy in 1902 and rose by 1936 to the rank of admiral and naval chief-of-staff. In 1939, he was given the unique title of "admiral of the fleet" and put in supreme command of French naval forces. He was a firm supporter of Pétain and in February 1941 became Pétain's deputy and effective head of the government. He collaborated with the German occupiers, and in May 1941 agreed the Paris Protocols that gave substantial concessions to the Germans in French Africa and the Middle East. In April 1942, the Germans, uncertain of Darlan's reliability, pressured Pétain to replace him with Laval. Darlan remained commander-in-chief of French forces. On 7 November he arrived in Algiers to visit his sick son and was caught up in the "Torch" invasions. He changed sides, agreed to a French ceasefire, and was declared high commissioner for French North Africa, but on 24 December he was assassinated by a French royalist resistance fighter, Fernand de la Chapelle, who was executed two days later.

GUADALCANAL

LEFT A Japanese ship in the major base at Rabaul is hit by a bomb from the US 5th Army Air Force during an attack. Air attack on the base neutralized it as a threat throughout the conquest of the Solomons and the other southwest Pacific islands.

BELOW LEFT A group of American servicemen celebrate Christmas midnight mass at an improvised service on Guadalcanal, 23 December 1942.

The battle for Guadalcanal reached a critical point by November 1942. Though on a scale very much smaller than the battles in the North African desert or around Stalingrad, the struggle for the island came to be regarded by both sides as a vital testing ground for American resolve on the one hand and Japan's capacity to protect her new-won empire on the other.

Japanese forces on the island were strengthened after the failure of the October assault on the American-held Henderson airfield by men shipped in Japanese naval vessels on the "Tokyo Express" supply route through the central Solomons. By 12 November the forces at the disposal of Lieutenant General Hyakutake exceeded American numbers for the first time – 23,000 against 22,000. But that same day a United States task force delivered reinforcements to Guadalcanal supported by air cover from aircraft carriers in the Coral Sea and heavy bombers on the island of Espiritu Santo. By early December the balance was once again in American favour, 40,000 troops against 25,000.

This situation might well have been reversed had it not been for a series of destructive naval battles off the northern coast of Guadalcanal between 12 and 15 November in which a United States task force tried to prevent further reinforcement. A large convoy of Japanese troops, heavily supported by naval vessels, arrived off Guadalcanal in Ironbottom Sound on the night of 12/13 November. A fierce ship-to-ship engagement followed which left six American ships sunk and cost the Japanese three, including a battleship. The following day American aircraft attacked the Japanese landing fleet, sinking a cruiser and seven transport ships. During the night of 14/15 November a second major naval engagement took place in which the

RIGHT A tired US soldier on his way back to Base Operations camp on Guadalcanal, February 1943, after 21 days of continuous combat. The fighting conditions for both sides were exceptionally tough throughout the island campaign.

REAR ADMIRAL RAIZO TANAKA (1892–1969)

A career officer in the Japanese navy, Tanaka became an expert on torpedoes in the 1920s and taught at the navy's torpedo school. In September 1941 he was appointed to command Destroyer Squadron 2 and in October promoted to rear admiral. He fought in the invasion of the Philippines and the Dutch East Indies. During the Solomons campaign Tanaka's destroyer force supplied Japanese forces on Guadalcanal along the "Slot" between the islands of the Solomons group. The Japanese called the supply runs "rat transportation", but the Allies nicknamed them the "Tokyo Express". Tanaka became critical of Japanese strategy and was redeployed to shore duties in Burma, where he remained for the rest of the war.

was replaced as commander by Major General Alexander Patch, commander of the Americal Division (a contraction of "American New Caledonian"). With more than 50,000 men under his command, he began a series of offensives against the poorly supplied Japanese. By this stage the Japanese navy command had decided that Guadalcanal would have to be abandoned and the Japanese Imperial Headquarters confirmed this decision on 31 December. The isolated Japanese forces fought with suicidal determination but were pressed back to the north of the island. Unknown to the Americans, Japanese destroyers off the coast successfully evacuated 10,650 troops, including Hyakutake, between 2 and 8 February, leaving Guadalcanal in American hands.

Over 20,000 troops were lost, 860 aircraft and 15 warships. The United States Navy also lost heavily, but the ground troops suffered only 6,111 casualties, including 1,752 killed. This remarkable disparity in losses was to be repeated in the island battles across the Pacific. If the Battle of Midway had determined the limit of Japanese naval expansion, the failure at Guadalcanal decisively halted the onward march of the Japanese army.

ABOVE Two American soldiers of the US 32nd Division fire into a dugout near the port of Buna in New Guinea in the drive to expel the Japanese from southern Papua at the same time as the operations on Guadalcanal.

BATTLE FOR NEW GUINEA

While the struggle was continuing in Guadalcanal, a second battle was taking place in eastern New Guinea where the Japanese had landed on 22 July 1942 to try to seize Port Moresby and expel Allied forces from the island. They landed at Gona and Buna and marched inland to seize Kokoda, and by September were 40 kilometres (25 miles) from the port. Stiff Australian and American resistance and the crisis in Guadalcanal forced a Japanese retreat and on 15 November Kokoda was recaptured. On 9 December the Japanese lodgement at Gona was eliminated by the Australian army and on 1 January 1943 Buna was captured as well. Japanese failure in New Guinea was further evidence that the outer perimeter of the southern zone could not be made secure.

Japanese battleship *Kirishima* and a destroyer were sunk for the loss of three US destroyers. In the end only 2,000 troops could be landed, with virtually no military supplies. The battles of Ironbottom Sound marked the end of Japanese efforts to save the position on Guadalcanal. One further attempt was made when Rear Admiral Tanaka personally commanded his destroyer squadron on 30 November in a run to Guadalcanal. His eight destroyers were surprised by a larger American force of five cruisers and four destroyers in Ironbottom Sound, but Tanaka's skilful handling of his ships produced a salvo of torpedoes that sank one cruiser and crippled the remaining three, before Tanaka retreated back up the Slot. The Battle of Tassafaronga, as it was known, was a tactical victory, but no supplies reached the embattled Japanese garrison.

In December 1942 the 1st Marine Division was replaced on the island by the 25th US Infantry Division and Vandegrift

ABOVE (BOX) An Australian mortar crew fire on the Japanese defenders of their stronghold of Buna, New Guinea, 8 February 1943. The Australians took the objective, one of the last held by the enemy in the area of the island.

RIGHT Japanese prisoners, sick and hungry, are taken down to the beach by American troops after the capture of a Japanese stronghold on Guadalcanal, 22 February 1943. Most Japanese troops had been evacuated to safety by this time.

OPERATION "URANUS"

12 NOVEMBER 1942
British Commonwealth forces retake Tobruk as they pursue Rommel in North Africa.

25 NOVEMBER 1942
Launch of Operation "Mars" against German Army Group Centre results in heavy Soviet losses.

30 NOVEMBER 1942
Battle of Tassafaronga when an inferior Japanese naval force inflicts heavy losses on the US Navy in the Guadalcanal campaign.

11 DECEMBER 1942
Hitler insists that the surrounded 6th Army must remain where it is in Stalingrad.

ABOVE Soviet order of the Red Star.

The view from Moscow in the autumn of 1942, as German forces pressed into Stalingrad and across the Caucasus region, threatening to cut the Volga and seize Soviet oil, looked increasingly desperate. Stalin and many of his senior commanders still assumed that German forces were planning a third operation to take the Soviet capital, and kept the largest part of the Red Army and air force along the front defending Moscow. On 27 August, Stalin finally summoned Zhukov, who had saved Leningrad and Moscow, and appointed him deputy supreme commander with the task of saving Stalingrad.

Zhukov visited the besieged city and returned to Moscow in mid-September. In conference with Stalin, Zhukov and the army chief-of-staff, Alexander Vasilevsky, hinted at a radical solution for saving the city. Stalin sent them away with instructions to bring back a definite plan. They returned with the outline for what became known as Operation "Uranus" – the first time the Soviet command had given a name to an operation. The object was to create a large reserve force north and south of Stalingrad and then to attack and sever the long, extended German flank, encircling Paulus in the city. Stalin approved, and during October and early November the Red Army, utilizing an elaborate plan of deception and camouflage, built up a force of over one million men, 14,000 heavy guns, 979 tanks and 1,350 aircraft. The German commanders, although anxious that the long line of communications stretching across the steppe to Stalingrad was vulnerable, particularly as it was mainly

ABOVE Soviet soldiers armed with hand grenades attack an enemy position on the outskirts of the Stalingrad pocket. The "Uranus" campaign required Soviet forces to secure a front line on either side of the corridor carved through the Axis lines, facing west towards the Don river and east towards Stalingrad.

ABOVE Artillery and rocket fire from Red Army units in the attack on Romanian forces at the start of Operation "Uranus", 19 November 1942.

protected by Romanian, Hungarian and Italian troops of Germany's Axis allies, believed that the Red Army had no reserves available to mount any kind of extensive operation.

The date set for Operation "Uranus" was 19 November, but it was not the only element in the Soviet plan. A second operation, codenamed "Mars", was planned for the central front to attack the German Army Group Centre, still only 160 kilometres (100 miles) from Moscow, and drive it back from the key salient around Rzhev-Vyazma. This operation, originally intended for October, was launched on 25 November, six days after "Uranus". Zhukov took charge of it while the encirclement of Stalingrad was entrusted to Vasilevsky. "Mars" was a costly failure, with over 70,000 casualties for an operation that was unable to push the German army back and eliminate the threat to Moscow. It succeeded only to the extent that it prevented the redeployment of German forces southwards to help to stem the disaster that swept over the southern front.

On 19 November, Operation "Uranus" began when forces from General Vatutin's Southwest Front and Rokossovsky's Don Front surprised and swept aside the

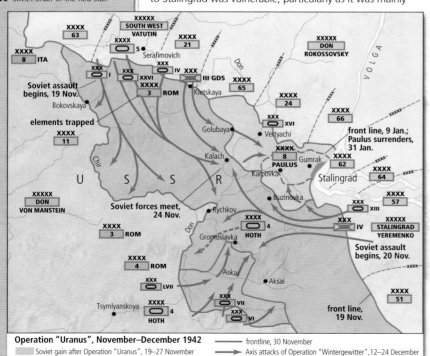

Operation "Uranus", November–December 1942
— frontline, 30 November
▭ Soviet gain after Operation "Uranus", 19–27 November
→ Axis attacks of Operation "Wintergewitter", 12–24 December

COLONEL GENERAL KURT ZEITZLER (1895–1963)

Zeitzler was chief of the army General Staff during the battle of Stalingrad. He joined the army in 1914 and was promoted to officer rank for bravery in the field. He became a career officer after 1919 and served as a staff officer, rising by 1939 to the rank of colonel and a position in the army High Command. He became chief-of-staff to von Kleist's Panzer Group A, and served under him in France, the Balkans and the Soviet Union. He became chief-of-staff of the 1st Panzer Army in October 1941, and was promoted on 24 September 1942 to chief of the army General Staff, jumping ranks to become a full general. He was appointed by Hitler as someone who would not be as critical as the more senior generals, but during the Stalingrad battle Zeitzler argued that Paulus should be allowed to break out of his encirclement against Hitler's orders. He was a reluctant chief-of-staff, and in July 1944 finally persuaded Hitler to let him retire on grounds of ill health. He retired from the army in January 1945. He was arrested after the war and held in British hands until his release in 1947.

MARSHAL ALEXANDER VASILEVSKY (1895–1977)

Vasilevsky was one of the architects of Soviet victory in the Second World War as chief of the Soviet General Staff from 1942 to 1949. The son of a priest, he worked as a teacher before joining the army in the First World War. He took up teaching again in 1918, but was drafted into the new Red Army and remained there. As a junior officer, he benefited from the Red Army purges of 1937. He was promoted to the General Staff in October that year, and two years later was deputy of the Operations Directorate, responsible for planning the war with Finland. He played a key role in the defence of Moscow, by which time he was commander of operations, and in April 1942 became acting chief of the General Staff, confirmed in June. He was instrumental in shaping the Red Army's defence at Stalingrad and in February 1943 was created marshal of the Soviet Union. He was liked by Stalin and suffered none of the problems after the war that other successful commanders faced, but his close links with the dictator led to his demotion in 1953 on Stalin's death and he never held another senior post.

Romanian 3rd Army, which surrendered two days later. On 20 November the southern wing, Yeremenko's Stalingrad Front, moved forward against the Romanian 4th Army, which disintegrated with the same speed. Stiffer resistance was met as the Red Army encountered German reserve forces, but the scale and surprise of the attack gave it a powerful momentum. By 24 November, the two prongs of the attack met at a village near the town of Kalach and the encirclement was complete. Soviet forces quickly established an outer and inner defensive ring so that a heavily armed corridor more than 160 kilometres (100 miles) wide separated Paulus's 6th Army from remaining Axis forces.

At this stage it was possible that Paulus might have successfully broken out of the trap and retreated towards the rest of the German forces further west. Hitler ordered him to hold fast, while the German air force commander, Hermann Göring, promised to supply Stalingrad by air with 500 tons of equipment and food a day. Field Marshal von Manstein was ordered to mount a rescue operation, codenamed "Wintergewitter" (Winter Thunderstorm),

which began on 12 December from the southwest of Stalingrad. Von Manstein, Paulus's front commander, ordered him to break out to meet him, but still bound by Hitler's instructions, Paulus failed to do so. In poor weather, von Manstein's force battled 65 kilometres (40 miles) towards Stalingrad but was then threatened with encirclement by a Soviet armoured attack and had to withdraw by 24 December. Operation "Uranus" had been a complete success. Stalingrad was surrounded while the Red Army began a second campaign, "Little Saturn", to push German forces in the south back across the Don steppe. By January, Paulus was more than 325 kilometres (200 miles) from friendly forces.

ABOVE A Soviet Cossack unit on horseback during Operation "Uranus". Cavalry remained an important element in the Red Army, allowing troops to move at speed over difficult countryside.

ABOVE Romanian POWs captured during Operation "Uranus" when the German 6th Army was encircled in Stalingrad. The Red Army calculated rightly that the Romanians would fight with less determination than the Germans.

BELOW Soviet soldiers in December 1942 on the outskirts of Stalingrad after the German forces in the city had been encircled. While some laid siege to the city, other forces moved westwards towards Kharkov.

DEFEAT AT STALINGRAD

10 NOVEMBER 1942
Admiral Darlan agrees to a general ceasefire in North Africa following "Torch" invasion.

2 JANUARY 1943
Allied forces capture the New Guinea port of Buna.

13 JANUARY 1943
Hitler issues his so-called "Total War" decree, calling for the highest sacrifices from the German people.

ABOVE One of the shoulder boards worn by Stalin after his appointment as Marshal of the Soviet Union in 1943.

The success of the Soviet Operation "Uranus" sealed the fate of an estimated 200–250,000 Axis troops in the Stalingrad pocket, including the 6th Army, most of the 4th Panzer Army and some units from Germany's Axis allies. Though there were stocks of ammunition and food in the city and three working airfields, supply to the trapped force failed to materialize on the scale promised. The airlift averaged less than 100 tons a day and the German air force lost 488 transport aircraft in the process. By January, food rations were down to 55 grams (two ounces) of bread a day and 28 grams (an ounce) of sugar. It was possible to fly out around 30,000 wounded men, but thousands of others suffering from frostbite and dysentery fought on from fear of what might happen to them or in the hope that rescue might be possible.

The Soviet High Command believed that the city contained only 80,000 of the enemy and that their exposed position would lead them to surrender. A force of 47 Soviet divisions was drawn up around the Stalingrad area, with 300 aircraft and 179 tanks to fulfil what was codenamed Operation "Kol'tso" (Ring). The attack was scheduled for 10 January, but Paulus was given the opportunity to surrender two days before, which he refused out of hand. Soviet planners expected the operation to last only a few days, but their miscalculation of the size of the trapped force resulted in a campaign of three weeks before the battle was over.

Operation "Kol'tso" began with the largest artillery barrage the Red Army had yet mounted. Paulus's forces

TOP Red Army motorized forces prepare for the final Stalingrad offensive late in 1942. After surrounding Stalingrad, Operation "Kol'tso" was mounted to destroy German resistance.

ABOVE The Soviet commander of the Don Army Group, Colonel General Rokossovsky, pictured in January 1943 shortly before the German surrender. Rokossovsky had been purged in 1937; allowed back into the army in 1940, he became one of the Red Army's most successful commanders.

RIGHT German soldiers unloading a plane inside the Stalingrad "cauldron". The only way they could be supplied was by air and by late January there was just one working airfield left, bringing in supplies and taking out the wounded and the mail.

VICTORY STATUE, VOLGOGRAD

In 1967 the remarkable statue "The Motherland Calls" was officially dedicated in a ceremony on the Mamayev Kurgan hill in the centre of Volgograd (formerly Stalingrad). Sometimes known as "Mother Motherland" or "The Motherland", the colossal statue was the tallest sculpture in the world, 85 metres (279 feet) high, with a vast sword some 33 metres (108 feet) long, and weighing 7,900 tons. From the foot of the hill 200 steps lead up to the monument, one for each day of the siege of Stalingrad. The principal sculptor was Yevgeny Vuchetich and the chief engineer was Nikolai Nikitin. The model for the statue was a native of Stalingrad, Valentina Izotova. The site was a symbolic recognition of the historic turning point in the war with Germany represented by the Battle of Stalingrad.

ABOVE German prisoners wearing rags and blankets to keep out the cold are marched through the streets of Stalingrad on their way to camps. A total of 91,000 prisoners were taken but many failed to survive the journey.

ENCLOSURES

1. A propaganda leaflet dropped on German forces in the Soviet Union in the last months of the war carries the assurance from Field Marshal Friedrich Paulus, the German commander captured at Stalingrad, that German prisoners will be treated "humanely and correctly". German sources estimate that over 1,000,000 Germans died in Soviet captivity.

2. The proclamation issued and signed by Adolf Hitler on 26 November 1942 to the troops of the German 6th Army and 4th Panzer Army trapped in the pocket at Stalingrad. Hitler promised to do everything in his power to help his forces in their "heroic struggle" but by 2 February 1943 all German resistance ended.

3. Summary of operations of November 1942–March 1943 drafted by Stalin and broadcast to the Soviet people, which covers the successful Operation "Uranus" that encircled German forces at Stalingrad and led to the first major German defeat.

MARSHAL ALEXANDER NOVIKOV (1902–76)

A career infantry officer from 1919, Novikov switched to the air force in 1933 as a very young chief of operations, but fell foul of the purges in 1937, when he was expelled from the armed forces. Reinstated, by 1939 he was chief-of-staff of the air force in the Leningrad Military District and a year later promoted to major general. A talented and creative military thinker, in April 1942 he was appointed commander-in-chief of the Soviet air force. He reorganized air forces into independent air divisions and corps and greatly improved air–ground co-ordination. His forces played an important part in eliminating the Stalingrad pocket, destroying around 1,200 German aircraft. After the war, he began to plan the postwar Soviet air force, but in April 1946 he was arrested, stripped of his rank, tortured into confessing absurd crimes and sent to a Gulag camp for 15 years. He was released in 1953 on Stalin's death and reinstated. He retired in 1956 to head the Civil Aviation School.

were stretched out in open country around Stalingrad as well as in the ruins of the city. The steppe was quickly cleared, reducing the pocket to half its original size within a week. But the Soviet forces found fighting amidst the urban ruins as difficult as the Germans' experience of it. In the heart of the city General Chuikov's 62nd Army was still fighting its own battle, turned now from defender into attacker by the success of the encirclement. His army pushed German troops back from the riverfront block by block. On 22 January, Soviet armies grouped for a final push into the city. Isolating each quarter at a time, they eliminated remaining resistance. German soldiers began to surrender in large numbers. On 26 January, contact was finally made between Chuikov's army and the vanguard of the attacking force near the Barricades Factory. By 31 January, Heroes of the Revolution Square, in the centre of the city, was finally reached.

Interrogators discovered that Paulus was sheltering in the Univermag department store on one side of the square. A young Soviet officer, Lieutenant Fyodor Yelchenko, was led into the basement of the building, where he found an unkempt and miserable commander. Paulus agreed to surrender and was taken away by car to Rokossovsky's

headquarters. In the north of the city, the remnants of the 4th Panzer Army fought a fierce final action, but were finally forced to surrender on 2 February. The defeat was the worst ever suffered by the German army. Some 91,000 went into captivity, but an estimated 147,000 had died in combat, or of frostbite, disease and hunger during the course of the battle. Soviet losses for the operations to encircle and destroy the Stalingrad pocket numbered 485,000, including 155,000 dead or captured.

Stalingrad was a signal that the tide had finally turned in the German-Soviet war. Most of the German army was still deep in the Soviet Union, stretched out along a 2,400-kilometre (1,500-mile front), but the contest between the two sides was no longer one-way. The victory reversed the long period of demoralization and uncertainty among Soviet leaders and the wider public. Stalin got himself appointed Marshal of the Soviet Union, his first military title. In Germany the defeat was greeted with disbelief and anxiety. Hitler, who had promoted Paulus to field marshal the day before the capitulation, was outraged that Paulus had not committed suicide. The day following German surrender, the radio repeatedly played "Siegfried's Funeral March" from Wagner's *Twilight of the Gods*.

BELOW The wreckage of a German unit in the battle for Stalingrad. The dead lay where they had fallen, left rigid by the extreme cold.

LEFT General Friedrich Paulus arrives at the Soviet headquarters to surrender formally on 31 January 1943.

THE CASABLANCA CONFERENCE

Between 14 and 24 January 1943, President Roosevelt and Prime Minister Churchill met in a hotel in a suburb of the French Moroccan city of Casablanca to discuss with the combined chiefs-of-staff (American and British) the future direction of western strategy once Africa was in Allied hands. Stalin was invited to the discussion but declined on the grounds that he was needed in Moscow to oversee the struggle in Stalingrad. Though this was true, Stalin also had a strong dislike of flying and obsessive concern with security.

The choice of Casablanca was Roosevelt's. Churchill had travelled extensively during the course of the war, but this was the President's first flight since assuming office in 1933 and he was keen to make a long overseas trip. He travelled by Pan-Am Clipper from Florida to The Gambia in

West Africa, and thence in a converted transport aircraft to Casablanca. He arrived with a large security detachment and travelled in a limousine with blacked-out windows. Churchill, in contrast, flew to Morocco in a noisy, cold converted bomber, which almost caught fire on the way. The two leaders arrived in an area that had only recently been liberated from Vichy French control; the conflict to eliminate the Axis presence enitrely in North Africa was reaching a climax at some distance along the Mediterranean coast in Tunisia.

During the course of 1942, high-level talks between the United States and Britain had revealed substantial differences in strategic perception. Roosevelt and his army chief-of-staff, George Marshall, were keen to see American troops in combat as soon as possible in Europe, but faced strong pressure to divert resources to the Pacific theatre. The two allies had agreed to undertake a cross-Channel invasion in 1943, codenamed Operation "Roundup", but this had not satisfied the president or Stalin, who hoped for a second front in 1942. Operation "Torch" was a compromise to allow US troops to see action in 1942, but the campaign made it unlikely that "Roundup" would be possible in 1943, and it committed Americans to a Mediterranean strategy which Marshall was generally opposed to.

ABOVE Roosevelt and Churchill pose for the camera with General Henri Giraud (left) and General Charles de Gaulle (second from right). The Americans wanted Giraud to become the leader of Free French forces in North Africa, but de Gaulle refused to be subordinated to a general with close links to Vichy.

LEFT A Moroccan newspaper vendor sells photographs of President Roosevelt during the Casablanca Conference in January 1943.

BELOW War correspondents at the Casablanca Conference in a press conference with Roosevelt and Churchill, the two figures who dominated the discussions.

CASABLANCA – THE FILM

The Hollywood film *Casablanca* was first screened in New York on 26 November 1942, two weeks after American forces entered Casablanca as part of the "Torch" landings in North Africa, and went on general release during the period of the Casablanca Conference. Directed by Michael Curtiz and starring Humphrey Bogart and Ingrid Bergman, the film became a propaganda vehicle for exposing the harsh realities of occupied and war-torn Europe. Most of the actors were European, many of them refugees themselves from Hitler's Germany or Austria, including Conrad Veidt who played National Socialist (Nazi) villains in this and other films. There were plans to change the film's now-famous ending by showing Bogart and a detachment of Free French soldiers on their way to invade North Africa but the idea was abandoned. Efforts to screen the film for troops in North Africa were prevented by the US Office of War Information in case it offended former Vichy officials.

GENERAL GEORGE C MARSHALL (1880–1959)

George Marshall was chief-of-staff of the United States Army and the senior military commander from 1939 to 1945. He provided a continuity of leadership found among none of the other combatant powers, and although his role was in an office rather than on the battlefield, his contribution to Allied victory was exceptional. Marshall was a born organizer whose value was observed in the First World War as chief of operations for the US 1st Infantry Division. He reached the rank of brigadier general by 1938 and became chief of the War Plans Division in Washington. The following year he was chosen by Roosevelt, above more senior candidates, as chief of the army staff. He spent the years before Pearl Harbor building up the American army and creating a framework for rapid mobilization. Favouring a "Germany first" strategy, he was instrumental in forcing through the idea of an invasion of northwest Europe. He became a five-star general in 1944 and retired from his post in November 1945. He was President Truman's secretary of state in 1947–49, during which time he launched the plan for the economic reconstruction of Europe that bore his name.

ABOVE A painting of German Propaganda Minister Joseph Goebbels addressing an audience at the Berlin Sportpalast, 30 January 1943, to mark the 10th anniversary of the Hitler regime. Responding to the Allies' demand for unconditional surrender, Goebbels made it into a propaganda tool to keep the German people fighting from fear of what might happen if they were defeated.

LEFT President Roosevelt (front left) talking to his close confidant Harry Hopkins on the return flight from the Casablanca Conference. The flight out had been Roosevelt's first trip in an aeroplane since becoming president in 1933.

RIGHT Winston Churchill sits in the sun in Marrakesh in Morocco convalescing after a bout of pneumonia in December 1943. Marrakesh was one of Churchill's favourite places, where he did much of his painting.

At Casablanca these differences were vigorously aired between the two leaders and the army chiefs-of-staff. Churchill and his chief-of-staff, General Alan Brooke, argued in favour of a Mediterranean strategy to attack Italy, which would compel the diversion of German forces and probably knock Italy out of the war. The campaign, they believed, would also weaken resistance in northern France and make an invasion there in 1943 or 1944 more likely to succeed. After a good deal of bitter argument, the American side accepted an invasion of Sicily, and reluctantly conceded that a major operation into France would have to be postponed until 1944.

These were not the only issues aired at Casablanca. Senior air force commanders also attended in the hope that they could persuade Roosevelt and Churchill to step up the bombing war as a substitute for a second front. Both men needed to be convinced, but the US commander-in-chief of the army air forces, Henry Arnold, together with Ira Eaker, commander of the US 8th Air Force in Britain, succeeded in presenting a compelling case. The Combined Bomber Offensive was agreed at Casablanca and a preliminary directive issued on 21 January for a campaign of round-the-clock bombing, the American air forces attacking by day, the RAF by night.

The most important outcome of Casablanca was the announcement at the final press conference of the principle of "unconditional surrender". Roosevelt used the phrase in his final remarks, but it was not repeated in the official communiqué from the conference. The issue had been discussed beforehand in Washington and in London, and Churchill was almost certainly unhappy about it since it tied British hands in their attempt to woo Italy away from the German alliance. Nevertheless, it became an immediate catchphrase and it bound the Allies to a policy of complete military victory, with no room for negotiation or armistice. Unconditional surrender has sometimes been criticized as too absolute a requirement but in the middle years of the war against powerful and implacable enemies it gave a clear statement of the minimum that the Allied powers expected from victory.

OPERATION "LONGCLOTH": CHINDITS IN BURMA

When combat came to an end in Burma (Myanmar) in 1942, a stalemate followed. The Japanese were too overstretched to attempt to penetrate any further, but British Indian forces in Assam needed to regroup, retrain and prepare thoroughly for warfare in the inhospitable conditions of Burma. An ill-prepared attack on the port of Akyab on the Burmese coast in autumn and winter 1942–43 ended in disaster, with no ground gained and 5,000 casualties.

The commander-in-chief in India, General Archibald Wavell, had invited Lieutenant Colonel Orde Wingate to India in March 1942 to prepare special forces for action behind Japanese lines. Wingate had served under Wavell in Palestine before the war and in East Africa in 1940–41. His force was officially designated the 77th Indian Infantry Brigade, but it was always known by the nickname "Chindits", derived from the Burmese word *chinthé*, a mythical winged lion, whose carved image was common on temples in Burma. Wingate developed the idea of long-range penetration operations using small units of specially trained men to infiltrate Japanese-held territory, cutting vital communication links and harassing the enemy. Although Wavell approved the tactic in principle, he was

ABOVE Major General Orde Wingate (centre, with hat) briefing men of the 77th Indian Infantry Brigade at an airfield at Sylhet in Assam before an operation. The forces that Wingate led into Burma had to be supplied entirely from the air.

BELOW Chindit soldiers with mules trekking through the Burmese jungle. They had to carry with them everything they needed, but food was always scarce.

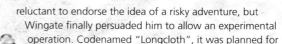

reluctant to endorse the idea of a risky adventure, but Wingate finally persuaded him to allow an experimental operation. Codenamed "Longcloth", it was planned for February 1943.

The Chindit force was organized into seven columns, each with between 400 and 500 men. The plan was to supply them from the air so that they could move with little equipment, and independent of any supply line. On the night of 14/15 February 1943, they crossed the Chindwin River into Burma, those columns commanded by Wingate moving north, and two columns heading southeast towards the Irrawaddy river. They succeeded in crossing large areas of the country and destroyed railway lines and bridges, but

they also encountered Japanese forces, fighting at least nine engagements. Air supply was difficult to organize, and the Chindits found themselves short of food and supplies and crippled by disease. Instead of moving to the planned area of operation for the period up to May around the town of Pago, they were ordered to make their way back to India in late March.

Out of the original 3,000 men, some 818 were dead or prisoners-of-war, and many of the rest too ill to continue. The operation achieved little in strategic terms, but it did act to boost morale in the Indian army, by showing that Japanese troops were not invincible. Wingate also won Churchill's admiration and the small guerrilla force became temporary heroes. Wingate was invited to attend the Quebec Conference in August 1943, where generous

MAJOR GENERAL ORDE WINGATE (1903–44)

Orde Wingate was one of the most unorthodox officers in the British army. A regular officer who served in Palestine in the 1930s, where he became a Zionist, he joined SOE (Special Operations Executive) and in the East African campaign in early 1941 formed "Gideon Force", an irregular guerrilla unit which fought in Ethiopia with the exiled emperor, Haile Selassie. He was virtually dismissed for insubordination after the campaign, and attempted suicide. In 1942, he was summoned by General Wavell to India to organize guerrilla combat against the Japanese in Burma. His "Chindit" force fought in 1943 and again in 1944, but he was killed in an air crash on 24 March 1944 before the second campaign had got very far. He had a mixed reputation. Rude, opinionated and irreverent, he also inspired loyalty among his men and the strong support of Winston Churchill, who liked his unconventional view of warfare.

MERRILL'S MARAUDERS

After the first Chindit campaign, an American force was raised to fight the Japanese in Burma using the same methods. The 3,000-strong force was codenamed "Galahad"; its official title was 5307 Composite Unit, but it was known as "Merrill's Marauders" after the group's commander, Brigadier General Frank Merrill. It trained with the Chindits, and was then assigned to work with the American General Joseph Stilwell and his Chinese forces in an operation against Japanese forces in northern Burma between February and August 1944. Despite early successes, the unit, like the Chindits in 1943, suffered from heavy losses, particularly due to disease and the arduous conditions in which they had to fight. In the end the force was decimated and at the end of the campaign was disbanded, its surviving members absorbed into the regular US army.

ABOVE Merrill's Marauders in action in the Pacific jungle, December 1943.

funds and equipment were put at his disposal. The operation also prompted the Japanese military to accept the need for a pre-emptive campaign of their own, which they launched in March 1944 against the towns of Imphal and Kohima in Indian Assam.

A second Chindit operation, codenamed "Thursday", was organized in February 1944 with some 20,000 special forces, designed to impede the Japanese assault on India. But Wingate's death in an air crash in March led to the abandonment of his irregular, deep-penetration tactics and the force fought in conventional formation alongside the forces of General Stilwell and elements of the Chinese army. This campaign also proved costly, with 3,628 casualties among the original Chindit force. The force was wound up in February 1945. Although their military achievements were modest, the Chindit campaigns were a model of heroism and endurance.

ABOVE A Chindit column crossing a river somewhere in Burma. They were organized into small self-contained groups to operate behind the lines. They all marched at least 1,000 miles during Operation "Longcloth".

ABOVE LEFT Formation badge of the 3rd Infantry Division – the Chindits.

BELOW Chindit forces prepare to blow a railway line far behind Japanese lines in Burma. They cut the main Mandalay–Lashio link before returning to India in March 1943.

ENCLOSURES
1. Notes for the training of special forces drawn up by Major General Orde Wingate in 1943 following the experience of the first Chindit operations in Japanese-controlled territory in Burma.
2. Family photographs of Sergeant Ken Wyse, captured on a Chindit operation in April 1943, on the back of which his colleague, Flight Lieutenant J K Edmonds, records Wyse's capture, subsequent mistreatment and death in a prison camp in Rangoon on 21 August 1943. Edmonds survived the war as a prisoner of the Japanese and returned the photos and wallet they were kept in to Wyse's family.

THE END OF THE AXIS IN AFRICA: TUNISIA

6 MARCH 1943
Stalin is named marshal of the Soviet Union and aquires a handsome new uniform.

13 APRIL 1943
Germans reveal the Katyn massacres of Polish officers by the Soviet security service, carried out in 1940.

18 APRIL 1943
Japanese Admiral Yamamoto, commander of the Japanese navy, is shot down and killed by US fighter aircraft on a flight over the Solomons.

23 APRIL 1943
Allies set up a planning centre in London under General Morgan to prepare the invasion of Europe in 1944.

ABOVE Badge of the British 78th Infantry Division.

After the success of the Second Battle of Alamein and the "Torch" landings in North Africa, the Allies had hoped to complete the elimination of enemy resistance within weeks. Instead Rommel successfully brought his battered Afrika Korps back to southern Tunisia by the end of January 1943, while in the north the 5th Panzer Army and the remnants of the Italian 1st Army, despite shortages of equipment, oil and ammunition, established a new Axis front line running the whole length of Tunisia.

The Allied plan was to try to divide the northern force under General von Arnim from Rommel's forces in the south with a drive by the US 1st Armored Division to the coastal port of Sfax (Operation "Satin"). But shortages of supply led to the cancellation of "Satin", and instead von Arnim and then Rommel took the initiative in attacking the US 2nd Corps from the eastern Dorsale Mountains in central Tunisia. On 14 February, the American force was driven back to the Kasserine Pass, and there, on 20 February Rommel, some of whose forces had moved up from the southern Mareth Line, inflicted a heavy defeat on the retreating American army. German units pushed on beyond the pass, but by 22 February they were halted by British and American counterattacks. Rommel moved back through the mountains, and moved south to defend against an anticipated attack by Montgomery's 8th Army.

The baptism of fire for American forces against experienced German and Italian troops was a harsh one. Relations between the American, British and French forces

ABOVE Local inhabitants in Tunis leave the city during the spring of 1943 to avoid the final showdown between Allied and Axis forces which reached its peak in May.

LEFT Following an Allied air attack on Tunis, a French auxiliary policeman carries a wounded child to a first aid station. The civilian population was caught in the middle of a conflict they had not expected.

Map: Tunisia, March–May 1943

Allied forces from Operation "Torch" arrive in Tunisia, mid-Nov. 1942

Axis reinforcements by air and sea, Nov. 1942

Bizerta 7 May
VAERST
ARNIM
Tunis 7 May

Philippeville · Bône · Tabarca
BRADLEY
V

XXXXX 18 ALEXANDER · XXXX 1 ANDERSON
IX

Constantine

Rommel invalided to Germany (Arnim assumes command), 6 Mar.

1 MESSE

Le Kef
KOELTZ

Atlas Mountains
ALGERIA

Enfidaville

Sousse 12 Apr.

Kairouan

Mediterranean Sea

Kasserine Pass, 14–22 Feb.
Tebessa
II PATTON
Kasserine

AFRIKA CORPS

Maknassy

Sfax 10 April

Eighth Army and "Torch" troops meet, 7 Apr.
Gafsa
Tozeur · El Hamma
1 MESSE
Gabès

Wadi Akarit, 6–7 Apr.
AFRIKA CORPS
Fortified line at Mareth assaulted, 20 Mar.

Chott Djerid

Mareth
Medenine
Ben Gardane
LIBYA
8 MONTGOMERY
NZ
X

Flanking movement by New Zealand Corps forces Axis forces to retreat, 22 March.

Tunisia, March–May 1943
salt marshes
— · — front line, 26 February
—— front line, 22 April

COLONEL GENERAL HANS-JÜRGEN VON ARNIM (1883–1962)

The son of a Prussian general, von Arnim joined the German army in 1907, fought in the First World War on the Western and Eastern fronts, and in the 1920s became commander of the elite 68th Infantry Regiment. He commanded divisions in Poland and France, and commanded the 17th Panzer Division for the invasion of the Soviet Union. He was seriously wounded a few days into the campaign, but by November 1942 had risen to command a Panzer corps. He was sent to North Africa to command the 5th Panzer Army and promoted to colonel general. When Rommel was invalided in March, he took over command of the Afrika Korps. He was captured by Indian troops in May 1943 and asked to be taken to Eisenhower. The Allied commander refused to meet any senior German officer until final surrender. Von Arnim was released in 1947.

MARSHAL GIOVANNI MESSE (1883–1968)

Marshal Messe was generally regarded as one of the most successful of Italian commanders in the Second World War. He joined the army in 1901, served in the Italo-Turkish war in 1911–12, and fought in the First World War, during which he was decorated for exceptional bravery and promoted to lieutenant colonel. He saw service in the Ethiopian war as a deputy divisional commander and in 1936 was promoted to general in command of the 3rd Mobile Division. He saw service in Albania in 1939 and in the Italian-Greek war in 1940–41. In July 1941, he was appointed commander of the Italian expeditionary force for the Eastern Front and fought in the battles on the Don towards Stalingrad, but was sent back to Italy in November 1942 for questioning Italian strategy. In February, he was sent to command Italian forces in Tunisia. He was promoted to Marshal of Italy on 12 May, and surrendered the following day. After the Italian surrender in September 1943, Messe was freed and returned to Italy to become chief of the Italian General Staff on the Allied side.

ENCLOSURES

1. A safe-conduct pass for Italian soldiers fighting in North Africa dropped over Italian forces during the campaign in Tunisia early in 1943 to encourage their surrender. "You can no longer escape from the vice" reads the headline.

2. General Montgomery's personal message to the troops of the 8th Army on the eve of the battle of Medenine on the Mareth Line in southern Tunisia on 2 March 1943. The following day Rommel ordered an attack but it was repelled and three days later Rommel was invalided back to Germany. Montgomery demanded "NO SURRENDER" and wished his troops "good hunting".

3. A proclamation issued by Lieutenant General Eisenhower late in 1942 announcing that the rule of Vichy France in French North Africa was ended and the local civilian population had to obey the orders of the US Army. Following German occupation of Vichy France in November, most French officials in North Africa complied with Allied demands.

were strained and supplies were difficult to bring across the long North African routes in poor weather and mud. Eisenhower appointed General Alexander to restore order to the Allied front and complete the destruction of the Axis pocket. Much depended on Montgomery breaching the Mareth Line, but in early March Rommel launched his own offensive. On 6 March, three Panzer divisions moved forward, but Montgomery, warned in advance by decrypted German messages, had prepared a trap. Rommel's tanks ran into a wall of withering anti-tank fire and were forced to retreat. On 9 March, Rommel flew to see Hitler to demand more assistance, but instead he was ordered on sick leave, his command taken by von Arnim.

On 20–21 March, Montgomery attacked with the bulk of the 8th Army against the Mareth defences, while the New Zealand Division was sent in a wide outflanking movement through hilly country to capture El Hamma in the Axis rear. Poor weather made progress slow in the frontal assault, and further armour was sent on the flanking attack. To the north, Alexander ordered the US 2nd Corps to drive for the coast and cut off the Axis retreat. The assault proved too difficult, and when Axis forces were compelled in late March to abandon the Mareth Line, they moved northwards, pursued by the 8th Army until they met up with the remaining German and Italian

forces in the north of the country. On 7 April, 8th Army troops met up with American forces coming from the northwest.

Von Arnim and the Italian commander, Marshal Messe, organized a final stand in the northeast corner of the country around Bizerta and Tunis. They judged their position to be hopeless, but after a meeting between Hitler and Mussolini in Salzburg on 8 April, they were ordered to hold fast at all costs. Supply was down to a fraction of what was needed. In three weeks in April, Allied fighter aircraft destroyed 432 Axis planes for the loss of just 35, including half the entire German air transport fleet. Axis forces had just 150 tanks, against more than 1,500 on the Allied side. Alexander ordered the American 2nd Corps to the north opposite the port of Bizerta; the British 1st Army under Lieutenant General Kenneth Anderson stood opposite Tunis; while the 8th Army occupied the southern section of the Allied noose. On 6 May, a general offensive was launched. Bombarded from the air and artillery, short of almost all essential supplies, Axis resistance collapsed. Bizerta and Tunis fell on 7 May, and five days later von Arnim, who had retreated to the very furthest tip of Tunisia on Cape Bon, surrendered. Marshal Messe, further south, surrendered to Montgomery a day later with the scattered remnants of his 1st Italian Army. Some 240,000 prisoners were taken, a defeat that ranked in numbers with Stalingrad three months before.

BELOW An American M3 Grant tank patrolling the streets of the Tunisian port of Bizerta, 8 May 1943. The city had fallen to the US II Corps the day before.

LEFT A wounded British soldier shares a cigarette with a captured German soldier during the battles for the Mareth Line in southern Tunisia in March 1943. In the end 125,000 Germans were captured in Tunisia.

BELOW General von Arnim, the German commander in Tunisia after Rommel's departure to Germany on health grounds, shortly after the Axis surrender on 12 May 1943.

THE DAMBUSTERS RAID

The decision to attack the major dams in the German Ruhr valley originated with the development of a "bouncing bomb" by the British engineer Barnes Wallis, who was convinced that attacking Germany's water supply would have a crippling effect on production and morale. The drum-shaped bomb was designed to rotate at speed as it was dropped from no more than 28 metres (60 feet) and then bounce across the surface of the water until reaching the dam wall, when it would spin to the foot of the wall and explode. The bomb was extensively tested and found to be a viable design. There then followed efforts to persuade the Air Ministry that an operation against the dams would work.

In Bomber Command there was a prejudice against what the commander-in-chief Arthur Harris called "panacea targets". The strategy pursued during 1942 and 1943 was to attack major industrial cities in order to reduce German economic capability, rather than attack a particular industrial or utility target. Harris finally agreed and aircraft were released to form what was called at first "Squadron X", but became designated 617 Squadron. The plan to bomb

ABOVE The production of shells in a factory in the Ruhr industrial region in 1942. The attack on the dams was supposed to undermine armaments production but it had very little direct effect.

LEFT An aerial reconnaissance photograph of the Möhne Dam taken before the Dambusters Raid. Together with the Sorpe Dam, the reservoirs supplied 75 per cent of the water needed by Ruhr industry.

RIGHT Three separate frames show an aircraft of 617 squadron practising dropping the "bouncing bomb" at the Reculver bombing range in Kent, southern England.

BARNES WALLIS (1887–1979)

A British aeronautical engineer, Barnes Wallis was responsible for developing a number of different aircraft and bomb designs during the Second World War. He joined the Vickers armaments company as a young engineer in 1913 and remained with the firm until his retirement in 1971. He designed the revolutionary geodesic airframe, first for airships, then in the Wellington bomber, an exceptionally sturdy aircraft capable of sustaining high levels of damage and still remaining airborne. He designed the bomb for the dams raid, and later the "Tallboy" and "Grand Slam" bombs for deep-penetration attacks. After 1945, he pioneered the "swing-wing" concept for fighter aircraft but saw his ideas developed first by American aircraft producers.

the dams was accepted on 26 February 1943, and there followed an intensive period of training in low-altitude flying and the use of the bouncing bomb, codenamed "Upkeep". A special aiming device was developed to ensure that the bomb was released at the right moment, and spotlights placed in the nose and tail of the Lancaster bombers used for the raid to provide a guide to altitude. By early May, the preparations were complete.

The operation, codenamed "Chastise", was undertaken on the night of 16/17 May 1943. The attacking force was organized into three groups: Formation 1 was to attack the Möhne Dam and, if there were bombs left, proceed to the Eder Dam; Formation 2 was to attack the Sorpe Dam; and a third reserve formation was to take off later and

WING COMMANDER GUY GIBSON (1918–44)

The commander of RAF 617 squadron was Wing Commander Guy Gibson. He joined the RAF in 1936 and on the outbreak of war was a pilot in 83rd Squadron, Bomber Command. He survived his first tour of duty and then transferred to Fighter Command where he flew night-fighters. He rejoined Bomber Command in 1942, flying the new Lancaster bombers, and was chosen in early 1943 to command the unit created to attack the German dams. He flew a remarkable 174 operations with Bomber Command, but was killed when his aircraft developed a fuel fault and crashed in the Netherlands on 19 September 1944. He had a reputation for tough professionalism and bravery and took risks other pilots might not have taken. He was awarded the Victoria Cross for his role in the destruction of the dams.

attack any dams that had not yet been breached. On the outward flight, the first formation lost one aircraft, while of the five aircraft in the second formation only one survived to reach the target: two were forced back and two were destroyed. The attack on the Möhne Dam was carried out successfully and the five surviving aircraft then flew to the Eder Dam, which was shrouded in fog. The final bombing run successfully breached the target. Formation 2 now consisted of one aircraft, whose bomb hit the Sorpe Dam but did not destroy it. Unlike the first two targets, the Sorpe was not made of concrete but of earth. Reserve aircraft then attacked but no further damage was caused.

The raid resulted in the loss of 11 bombers out of 19 and the loss of 53 out of 133 crewmen. The effect of the raids proved a disappointment to the planners. A huge area of flooding around 80 kilometres (50 miles) in length killed an estimated 1,650 people (including 1,026 POWs and foreign forced labourers) and inundated farmland. But Ruhr industry was hardly affected, electricity supplies were soon restored, and by 27 June there was a full water supply again. German authorities were alarmed by the prospect of a sustained attack against the Reich's water supply, but the operation

was not repeated and Bomber Command returned to the strategy of area bombing. Harris remained unconvinced of the value of attacking a single target-system, and was later unenthusiastic about the transportation and oil plans developed in the summer and autumn of 1944 as the key to speeding up German collapse. 617 Squadron was kept in being for specialist operations, however, and was later used to carry Barnes Wallis's super-heavy bombs which sank the German battleship *Tirpitz* and penetrated the six-metre (20-foot) reinforced concrete roofs of the submarine pens at Brest.

The operational success of the attack on the dams was exploited for propaganda purposes. Guy Gibson, the commander of the operation, was sent on a publicity tour of the United States and the raid attracted a high level of attention in Britain in the summer of 1943. Nevertheless, its strategic worth was limited and the cost in skilled crewmen very great. There was also discussion of its moral implications, which almost certainly made further similar attacks difficult to justify. In postwar international law the deliberate attack of civilian water supplies has been prohibited.

LEFT Wing Commander Guy Gibson and his crew board their Lancaster bomber for the attack on the dams, 17 May 1943. He was one of the lucky ones to return.

LEFT Albert Speer (left), the German minister for weapons and munitions, visiting the Möhne Dam after its destruction by RAF 617 Squadron. Emergency water supplies could be found within days of the attack and the dams were repaired rapidly thereafter.

BELOW Water pours through the broken dam wall of the Möhne Dam after the successful attack. The result was a flood extending some 80 kilometres (50 miles).

RATIONING: THE WAR FOR FOOD

4 SEPTEMBER 1939
German War Economy Decree introduces comprehensive rationing scheme in Germany.

8 JANUARY 1940
Britain introduces ration books for all consumers. Bacon, butter and sugar were the first items to be rationed.

3 JULY 1954
Meat is the last foodstuff to be de-rationed in Britain.

ABOVE Soviet poster urging the collective farms to produce more for the war effort – "More grain for the front and home front! Harvest as much as you can!"

One of the chief lessons of the First World War was the need to supply the home population with adequate food supplies. The Russian war effort collapsed in revolution partly on account of widespread hunger in the towns; the German war effort was undermined by the harsh "turnip winter" in 1917–18 when the urban population experienced real deprivation. In the 1930s, when the prospect of war loomed once again, governments began to plan the effective rationing and distribution of food to make sure that the home front did not suffer from the consequences of war. In Germany and Italy a programme of "self-sufficiency" was introduced to make both countries less dependent on imported food.

During the war, the supply of food became a critical issue once more. Germany and the areas it had conquered were cut off from all overseas sources of supply. Food of all kinds was rationed from the outbreak of war in Germany, leaving most consumers reliant on a limited range of bread, flour and potatoes, with meat and sugar in small quantities. The ration was maintained only by the ruthless requisitioning of food from occupied Europe, where ration levels were in general below those in Germany. In Britain the problem was an excessive dependence on overseas sources of supply. During the war, British agriculture was transformed, with large increases in arable land and a sharp reduction in livestock farming. Some 2.8 million hectares (7 million acres) of grassland were ploughed up and wheat, potato and barley production doubled. The result was a reduction

ABOVE Girls from the Women's Land Army dig out a bog oak from a piece of reclaimed fenland in Cambridgeshire, England. The organization had been used in the First World War and was revived in 1939. However, most farmworkers, even by the end of the war, were men.

RIGHT Poster featuring "Dr Carrot", created by Britain's wartime Ministry for Food to encourage people to make full use of the relatively plentiful carrot.

BELOW The English town of Cheltenham set up bins for scrap food during the war to be fed to pigs. The collections produced 20 tons of pig food every week.

DOCTOR CARROT the Children's best friend

of food imports by 50 per cent. Rationing was introduced for a range of basic foodstuffs, providing a diet not very different from the German one. It was possible, nevertheless, to buy more goods off the ration in Britain than was the case in Germany. Although a black market existed for those who could afford the prices, the authorities clamped down more harshly on irregular trade than had been the case in the First World War.

In the Soviet Union and the United States, the food situation was very different. America was a food-rich economy and, while a few foods were rationed to ensure a regular supply for all consumers, the impact of rising living standards during the war meant that many Americans ate better than they had done in the 1930s. Food was exported in large quantities to both the Soviet Union and Britain.

TO SAVE YOUR BACON SAVE YOUR SCR...

PIG FOOD

HERBERT BACKE (1896–1947)

Herbert Backe was the acting minister for agriculture in Hitler's government, and from 1944 minister for food. His trader father lived in Russia before 1914 and Backe was interned as an enemy alien throughout the war. During the Russian Civil War, following the Revolution, he escaped to Germany and became an agricultural specialist. He joined the National Socialist Party in 1923 and became one of the party's food experts. In October 1933, he became state secretary in the Agriculture Ministry charged with expanding German food production in case of war, making Germany more than 80 per cent self-sufficient by 1939. During the war he was made responsible for squeezing food out of the occupied Soviet Union and the so-called "Backe Plan" anticipated imposing widespread hunger on the Russian population. He was arrested after the war as a war criminal and hanged himself in his cell in Nuremberg on 6 April 1947.

The situation in the Soviet Union was disastrous. The German invasion conquered the Russian "bread basket" in the Ukraine, reducing the grain area by 40 per cent and livestock by two-thirds. Rationing was introduced in July 1941 in Moscow and by November had spread to the whole urban area (peasants were expected to make do with what they could grow on their garden plots). Food was exchanged for work and those who could not work, the elderly or infirm, relied on family help. An unknown number of non-workers perished of hunger in the first years of the war. Factory canteens were set up, feeding around 25 million workers with a hot meal. Land was distributed to workers as small allotments so that they could grow their own food and by 1944 there were 16.5 million of them. Soviet citizens also existed on a monotonous diet of bread, potatoes and occasional meat or sausage. But unlike the First World War, it proved possible to keep the population fed sufficiently not to endanger the domestic war effort.

ABOVE A customer shops in an American supermarket during the war. Food supplies were plentiful in the United States and large quantities of food were sent to America's allies.

DIGGING FOR VICTORY

During the Second World War, the British government promoted the idea of "digging for victory" by bringing gardens, parks, sports fields and unused land under cultivation. People were encouraged to run allotments and by 1944 there were 1.7 million of these, producing in 1943 an estimated one million tons of vegetables. The minister for food, Lord Woolton, set up an energetic propaganda campaign to encourage people to keep pigs, poultry and rabbits as well as grow vegetables. To make a vegetable diet more palatable, helpful recipe suggestions were published with the help of Dr Carrot and Potato Pete, two characters dreamt up by the propaganda department of Woolton's ministry. The big advantage of digging for victory was access to food off the rations.

FAR LEFT Lunch in a factory canteen in a British munitions factory. In order to encourage higher productivity, factories introduced welfare facilities, crèches for children and regular food not only in Britain but also in Germany, the United States and the Soviet Union.

LEFT A child begging for food in Calcutta during the Bengal famine, December 1943. Shortages of sea transport, needed for military operations, reduced the supply of food to the region and left an estimated 2–3 million dead.

Many of those recruited into the armed forces came from the countryside. Farm labour was not treated as a reserve occupation. Their place was taken by the elderly, by the young, and above all by women. In Britain a Women's Land Army was recruited, reaching a peak of 80,300 in December 1943, and constituted a large proportion of the 117,000 women working on British farms. But in Germany women had always made up a large part of the rural workforce on the small peasant farms, and by 1944 there were 5.7 million working in agriculture, around 38 per cent of all employed women. In the Soviet Union some 80 per cent of farm workers on the collective farms were women by the end of the war. They did all the jobs usually done by men, and did them in many cases without the help of machinery or draft animals, which had long ago disappeared to the front. To do this they had to make do with payment of one potato and 200 grams (seven ounces) of bread a day. They survived on only what they could grow around their cottages, or what they could steal. The efforts to mobilize the home front ensured that none of the combatant powers experienced a severe crisis of food supply, except for Japan in the last months of the Pacific War when bombing dislocated the whole supply system. Famine did occur – in Bengal in 1944, in Greece in 1943–44 and in the Netherlands in the last months before liberation – as a result of the exceptional circumstances of war. Hunger was more common after the war in the chaos of occupation and reconstruction.

THE BATTLE OF KURSK

29 JUNE 1943
Start of Operation "Cartwheel" designed to roll up Japanese resistance in New Guinea and the islands of the South Pacific.

5–6 JULY 1943
Battle of Kula Gulf off New Heorgia in the Solomons fails to prevent Japanese reinforcement.

10 JULY 1943
Operation "Husky", the Anglo-American invasion of Sicily, begins.

13 JULY 1943
Hitler orders redeployment of German forces to Italy to stem the Allied advance in the Mediterranean theatre.

24 JULY 1943
Start of the bombing campaign against Hamburg in Operation "Gomorrah".

25 JULY 1943
Mussolini is overthrown as Italy's dictator and is arrested.

After the disaster at Stalingrad it was necessary for the German army in the Soviet Union to win back the initiative. Between 29 January and 23 March, a series of battles took place around the city of Kharkov, the Soviet Union's fourth-largest city, reducing it to rubble in the process. An overstretched Soviet offensive was driven back past Kharkov by the forces of von Manstein's Army Group South (the renamed Army Group Don) as far as the city of Belgorod. This offensive created the southern side of a large Soviet salient, 190 kilometres (120 miles) wide and 95 kilometres (60 miles) long, bulging into the German front line around the city of Kursk. It was here that von Manstein and the army High Command decided the key battle of the summer 1943 campaign should be fought. The operation was codenamed "Zitadelle" (Citadel).

The German plan followed a predictable pattern. The object was to drive two heavily armed wedges into the neck of the salient from north and south to encircle and cut off the large Soviet forces stationed there. Victory here would allow German forces to swing either south again or to move behind Moscow and turn the Soviet line. A force of 900,000 men in 50 divisions, 2,000 aircraft and 2,700 tanks was assembled, including the new heavy Panther and Tiger tanks and the Ferdinand self-propelled gun. Hitler was uncertain about the operation and refused von Manstein's request to begin in May before the Red Army was ready. In the end, he postponed the start date until early July.

The interval gave the Soviet High Command plenty of time to prepare the battlefield. Zhukov and the General Staff guessed the German plan and won support from Stalin, who had wanted an immediate offensive, to build up a heavy defensive shield around Kursk prior to delivering a knock-out blow to the German attackers with large forces held in reserve. The Kursk salient was held by two army fronts, the central front under General Rokossovsky and the Voronezh front under General Vatutin, both of whom had led the defence of Stalingrad. They prepared six separate lines of defence and a complex wall of artillery and anti-tank fire was established. Into the defensive line were moved 1.3 million men, 3,444 tanks and 2,900 aircraft, around 40 per cent of Soviet manpower and 75 per cent of its armoured force. Both sides treated the huge set-piece battle as a test of strength; the loser risked a great deal.

The Soviet side needed to know when the blow would come, and they were supplied with a large amount of accurate intelligence, but because Hitler kept altering the date there could be no certainty. The "Lucy" spy ring in Switzerland gave the approximate date in early July, but

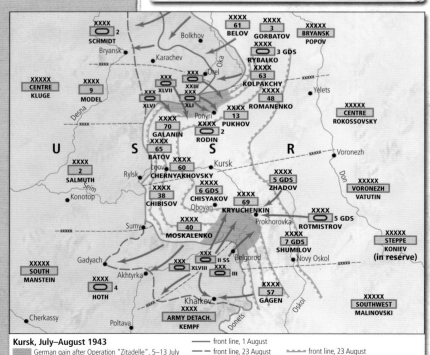

Kursk, July–August 1943

German gain after Operation "Zitadelle", 5–13 July

— front line, 1 August
– – front line, 23 August
· · · front line, 23 August

COLONEL GENERAL HERMANN HOTH (1885–1971)

The son of an army officer, Hoth joined the army in 1903, fought in the First World War in a variety of roles and stayed on in the postwar 100,000-man force. He rose rapidly during the period of the Third Reich. In October 1938, he commanded the 15th Army Corps and in November that year was made a general. He fought in Poland and France and commanded the 3rd Panzer Group in November 1940, which captured Minsk in the opening weeks of the invasion of the Soviet Union. In June 1942, he took over command of the 4th Panzer army and fought in the Stalingrad campaign, unsuccessfully leading the effort to rescue Paulus in December 1942. His Panzer group fought at Kursk and later failed to prevent the Soviet reconquest of Kiev, for which he was sacked by Hitler. A ruthless officer, he endorsed harsh measures against Jews and partisans and was convicted at Nuremberg in 1948 of war crimes. He served six years of his 15-year sentence.

ABOVE Soviet partisan fighters laying explosives on a railway line behind the German front during the Battle of Kursk, July 1943.

ABOVE LEFT German infantry and armoured forces during the Battle of Kursk in July 1943. The German army deployed the large Tiger and Panther tanks at Kursk for the first time. The Tiger carried a huge 88-millimetre (3.5-inch) gun, the Panther 75-millimetre (3-inch).

the final date and hour, dawn on 5 July, were found out from kidnapped German soldiers. The Red Army fired a number of pre-emptive artillery barrages during the night, but the attack went ahead as planned. In the south, General Hoth's 4th Panzer Army, with nine Panzer divisions, crashed forward against the weaker of the two Soviet fronts and in two days it was 30 kilometres (20 miles) towards Kursk, fighting against frantic and stiff opposition. In the north, General Walter Model's 9th Panzer Army was held almost at once by a withering wall of fire. On 6 July, 1,000 tanks were pushed forward on a front only 10 kilometres (six miles) wide towards the town of Ponyri, but by the following day the offensive was bogged down and by 9 July the German northern thrust was halted.

BELOW Soviet infantry run past a burning T34 tank during the Battle of Kursk. Despite heavy losses, the Red Army was able to blunt the German attack and push back the German front line in a series of powerful counter-offensives.

In the south, Hoth's Panzer army moved towards the small town of Prokhorovka where it met the 5th Guards Tank Army commanded by General Pavel Rotmistrov, which had travelled for four days to reach the battlefield. What followed on 12–13 July has usually been described as the largest tank battle of the war, but recent research has suggested that most of the casualties to the Soviet side were caused by Rotmistrov's failure to recognize a Soviet tank trap into which his unfortunate armour blundered. German losses were modest, but the failure in the north and news of the Allied landings in Sicily had led Hitler to cancel the operation on 13 July. Hoth retreated back to where he had started. German commanders failed to realize what would follow because they underestimated Soviet reserves. In the north on 12 July, a massive counter-offensive was launched which liberated Orel on 5 August and Bryansk on 18 August. In the south, the attack was launched on 3 August and by 28 August Kharkov was again in Soviet hands. The way was now open for a general summer offensive to drive back the whole German front.

ABOVE LEFT German tanks make their way across the steppe during the Battle of Kursk in July 1943. The confrontation was the largest concentration of tank forces yet seen in the war.

ABOVE A destroyed Soviet column during the Battle of Kursk. Although a Soviet victory, the losses of the Red Army amounted to 70,000 dead or captured.

ABOVE German tanks and soldiers at the heart of the battle in July 1943. German losses were much lower than Soviet, with an estimated 15,000 dead and the loss of only 300 tanks.

OPERATION "HUSKY": INVASION OF SICILY

12 JULY 1943
Red Army begins Operation "Kutuzov" against the German-held city of Orel following the end of "Zitadelle".

17 JULY 1943
Following Allied deceptive measures, Hitler orders reinforcements to go to Greece to resist an expected Allied invasion of the region.

1 AUGUST 1943
Japan declares Burma to be an independent state, though under close Japanese supervision.

5 AUGUST 1943
US forces complete the capture of New Georgia in the Solomons.

12 AUGUST 1943
A force of over 600 RAF bombers attacks the major Italian industrial centre of Milan.

ABOVE Badge of the British 6th Airborne Divisions.

It was agreed at the Casablanca Conference that the invasion of Sicily would follow the defeat of the Axis in North Africa. Planning began in the spring for Operation "Husky", which was assigned to General Alexander's 15th Army Group, made up of Montgomery's 8th Army and Patton's 1st US Armored Corps (renamed 7th US Army for the invasion). The object was to land in force on the southern and southeastern coast and to sweep up the island quickly enough to prevent Axis forces from escaping to the mainland. The date was set for 10 July 1943.

In order to render the ambitious amphibious operation more secure – it was second in size only to the later invasion of France – a risky deception plan was mounted codenamed Operation "Mincemeat" which involved leaving a dead body dressed in the uniform of a Royal Marines major off the Spanish coast with false Allied plans concealed in a

ABOVE An aerial view of the island of Pantelleria during a heavy Allied air bombardment in June 1943. The island was on the route to Sicily and the garrison had to be eliminated before the landings on Sicily could begin.

ABOVE The British 51st Highland Division unloading supplies on a beach in southeast Sicily on 10 July 1943 as part of the invasion force. There was little opposition at first against the British sector.

briefcase. The body was handed to the British consul, but the briefcase was kept by the Spanish authorities and its contents revealed to the German consul. The fake plan described an Allied operation against Greece with Sicily as a diversion. The ruse worked perfectly and German forces were strengthened in Greece and Sardinia, but not in Sicily.

Air power was to play an important part in the invasion. In June, an Italian garrison on the island of Pantelleria, lying on the route from North Africa to Sicily, was so pulverized by bombing that the garrison surrendered without an invasion. Aircraft neutralized any threat from Axis air forces during the invasion. On 9 July, the operation began with American and British paratroop landings to secure vital bridges and communications. Strong winds produced a disaster, with 200 British paratroopers drowning in the sea. Out of 2,781 US paratroops, only 200 arrived at the objective near the Sicilian port of Licata. During the night of 9/10 July, a flotilla of 2,590 ships and landing craft approached Sicily, carrying 180,000 men. They were faced by approximately 50,000 German and 270,000 Italian troops, but it was expected that most Italians would have little stomach for the battle.

British forces landed without difficulty on the beaches at Avola and Pachino, and US forces faced serious opposition only at Gela, where the Hermann Göring Division was stationed. Within five days, Allied forces had pushed inland to a line from Agrigento to the Gulf of Catania. Progress proved slow in mountainous terrain which gave every advantage to the defender against an armoured attack. Patton was supposed to protect the flank of the 8th Army as it struck north to Messina and northwest to the central Sicilian city of Enna, but the collapse of Italian resistance against his aggressive armoured drive persuaded him that the whole of the west of the island could fall quickly

GENERAL MILES DEMPSEY (1896–1969)

Dempsey was one of Montgomery's most successful 8th Army generals. He served with the Royal Berkshire Regiment in the First World War, and continued to do so in the interwar years. He fought in France in 1940, and as a lieutenant general was sent to command the 13th Corps of the 8th Army, which he led in North Africa, Sicily and Italy. He commanded the 2nd Army in the Normandy invasion and ended the war accepting the surrender of Hamburg in 1945. He became commander-in-chief Allied Land Forces in Southeast Asia, and was commander-in-chief in the Middle East in 1946–47 during the crisis in Palestine. He retired from the army in July 1947 and was commander-in-chief of UK Land Forces Designate from 1951 to 1955.

ABOVE The population of Palermo turn out to greet units of Patton's 7th US Army on 23 July 1943 after the surrender of the city. There was widespread enthusiasm in southern Italy for the end of hostilities.

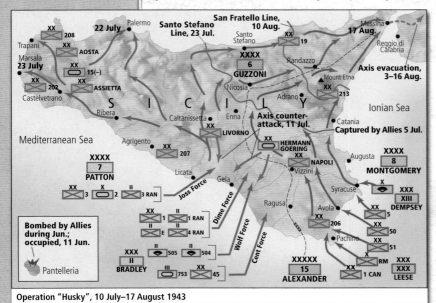

Operation "Husky", 10 July–17 August 1943

ABOVE Gunners of the British 66 Medium Regiment, Royal Artillery in action near the slopes of Mount Etna in northeast Sicily, 11 August 1943.

GENERAL GEORGE S PATTON (1885–1945)

One of the most controversial but successful of American generals during the Second World War, Patton joined the US cavalry in 1909, fought in Mexico in 1916 and in France in 1917–18, first on the staff of the US commander General Pershing, then in command of a tank brigade. In January 1942, he took command of the 1st Armored Corps. He commanded the western task force which landed at Casablanca in November 1942, and commanded the 2nd US Army Corps in Tunisia in March and April 1943, before being recalled to plan the invasion of Sicily. His public persona was flamboyant, aggressive and coarse, and he famously flaunted a pair of ivory-handled pistols, but he was also a scrupulous and hardworking commander. He made morale a high priority, but when he assaulted and abused two combat-weary soldiers in the Sicilian campaign to get them to carry on fighting, the incident almost ended his career. He was recalled to command the 3rd US Army in the Normandy invasion, and his aggression and operational awareness made him an outstanding armoured commander. He was made a four-star general in April 1945, but died in a car accident eight months later.

RIGHT A defaced portrait of Mussolini hangs on a lamppost in northern Sicily on the road from Messina to the coast, with German and Italian road signs beneath it. Mussolini fell from power on 25 July.

ENCLOSURES

1. A situation map of the early progress in Sicily of Operation "Husky" after the invasion on 10 July. By 15 July the line from Agrigento to Augusta had been reached and American forces fanned out into western Sicily. The British 8th Army made slower progress towards Catania. The map shows clearly how important naval gunfire was to the land operations along the Sicilian coastline.

2. The final plan for Operation "Husky", drawn up on 4–5 June 1943 following the defeat of Axis forces in Tunisia in May. Eisenhower remained the overall commander-in-chief while the British general, Harold Alexander took command of forces in the field.

BELOW The 380-millimetre (15-inch) guns of the British battleship HMS *Warspite* bombarding Axis forces holding the Sicilian port of Catania in the middle of July 1943. Naval fire played an important part in securing the landings in Sicily and later on mainland Italy.

into Allied hands. This was one of many arguments that continued to sour Anglo-American co-operation. Alexander reluctantly agreed, and Patton's units reached Palermo on 22 July.

Montgomery's progress proved frustratingly slow and Catania was taken only on 5 August. By this time, Alexander had ordered Patton's forces to swing east towards Messina to assist the 1st Canadian Division as it looped west of Mount Etna, on a trajectory initially assigned to the American zone. In the midst of the final push towards Messina, the Italian dictator, Benito Mussolini, was overthrown on 25 July 1943. Hitler, who had insisted

on no withdrawal, was compelled to order an evacuation across the Straits of Messina. The Italian army under General Alfredo Guzzoni saw little point in continued resistance. By the time Allied forces converged on Messina, over 100,000 Italian and German forces had successfully been removed, without any serious air or naval action by the Allies. Patton arrived in the centre of Messina two hours before the British on 17 August, but the trap had failed to be sprung and one-third of Axis forces escaped. The campaign cost the Allies 38,000 casualties, but approximately 200,000 Italian soldiers surrendered in the course of the campaign, no longer willing to fight for a cause that had collapsed.

THE BOMBING OF HAMBURG

In the spring of 1943, RAF Bomber Command chose Hamburg, Germany's second-largest city and a major port and manufacturing centre, for a sustained and destructive attack codenamed Operation "Gomorrah". The campaign was an opportunity to try out two tactical innovations. The first was a new navigation aid, the H2S radar scanning apparatus that provided an image of the ground, the second a device known as "Window" which would block German radar by distributing thousands of aluminium-coated foil strips to create a mass of confusing data on the radar screen. The orders for "Gomorrah" went out on 27 May and the campaign against Hamburg was scheduled to begin on 24 July.

The attack on Hamburg was planned as a series of operations to maximize destruction and dislocation and to make it difficult for the rescue and fire services to continue to operate effectively. It was a combined operation, the RAF bombing by night and the United States 8th Air Force by day against designated industrial and transport targets. The first attack came on the night of 24/25 July, when 791 bombers set out for the city, the last on the night of 2/3 August when 740 bombers were sent off from British bases. The bomber streams were led by a Pathfinder force which carried H2S equipment and whose task was to pinpoint the main bombing area with flares. During the first operation, around 2,300 tons of bombs were dropped, a mixture of incendiary and high explosive.

ABOVE American Boeing B-17 "Flying Fortress" bombers in formation on a mission over Germany. The heavily armed bomber formed the mainstay of the US 8th Air Force bomber squadrons stationed in England and was used in the raids on Hamburg on 25 and 26 July 1943.

LEFT Aerial image taken during the first raid on Hamburg. Sticks of incendiaries can be seen burning in the Altona and dock districts of they city. This first attack did not produce the terrible firestorm though it caused widespread damage.

BELOW German civilian dead line a Hamburg street after a bombing raid during the nine-day Operation "Gomorrah" which caused an estimated 45,000 civilian deaths.

ABOVE LEFT Door plaque for the German National Air Raid Protection League, equivalent of Britain's ARP.

The following afternoon, 123 American B-17 bombers attacked Hamburg, aiming for the main shipyards. On the night of 25/26 July a handful of British Mosquito bombers flew over Hamburg to create alarm and the following day a further American attack with 121 bombers was made against the port area.

Over the next two days further alarms sounded regularly as the Hamburg population began to leave the city to avoid the continuing threat. On the night of 27/28 July, RAF Bomber Command returned in force with 787 bombers, and it was this raid, which created the first bombing firestorm, that made the operation notorious. The firestorm, in the eastern districts of the city, was the result of the high proportion of incendiary bombs dropped and the difficulty faced by the rescue services, after three days of bombing, in tackling hundreds of fires in areas with blocked roads and disrupted water supplies. The fires gradually merged together and by 1.20 a.m. the storm began to develop, reaching a climax at around 3.00 a.m. with temperatures

LIEUTENANT GENERAL IRA C EAKER (1896–1987)

Ira Eaker became commander of the US 8th Air Force in 1943 and was a major architect of the United States's daylight bombing campaign over Germany. A farmer's son from Texas, Eaker joined the army in 1917 and was trained as an army pilot in 1918. He saw service in the Philippines in 1919–21 before returning to the United States where he took part in a number of endurance flights, winning the world flight endurance record in 1929. His career in the 1930s and early 1940s was with fighter aircraft, but in January 1942 he was assigned to organize the 8th Bomber Command based in England, and in February 1943 took over as commander of the 8th Air Force. He personally flew in the first US bombing mission over Rouen in August 1942. Criticism of high losses in 1943 led to his replacement in December, and he became commander-in-chief of Allied Mediterranean Air Forces. He became chief of the air staff in April 1945 and retired in 1947 as a lieutenant general. In 1985, President Reagan awarded him a retrospective general's fourth star.

of 1,800 degrees centigrade and winds of 240 kilometres (150 miles) per hour. Everything in the path of the firestorm was consumed and human bodies incinerated. In the cellars, where many people had fled, the heat literally melted their bodies. The firestorm was the most deadly bombing attack yet experienced and an estimated 40–45,000 people lost their lives in one night, the equivalent of all those killed in nine months of the Blitz against Britain.'

Even though Hamburg was now a skeleton city, the RAF returned on the night of 29/30 July, creating a smaller firestorm in the northeast of the city, and once more on the night of 2/3 August, although on this occasion heavy thunderstorms scattered the force and Hamburg suffered much less. On this final raid, the bomber force suffered its highest losses, 30 aircraft in total. Over the whole campaign the RAF dropped approximately 7,800 tons of bombs on Hamburg for the loss of 87 bombers, while the two 8th Air Force raids cost 17 bombers. The damage to the city was extensive: 25 square kilometres (10 square miles) of the city were obliterated, leaving over one million people homeless. Half the city's 81,000 commercial and industrial buildings were destroyed and over 40,000 residential buildings. Losses also included 58 churches, 277 schools and 24 hospitals. Besides the 45,000 dead were 37,439 with serious injuries.

The economic impact on Hamburg was, however, much less than Harris and Bomber Command had hoped. By the end of 1943, Hamburg's industrial production had reached 82 per cent of the pre-raid level. Much of the damage had been to residential areas, but local war industries, while temporarily disrupted by the exodus of workers from the city, were quickly restored or dispersed to safer sites. Albert Speer, the German armaments minister, thought that six similar attacks would knock Germany out of the war, but Bomber Command proved unable to replicate "Gomorrah".

ABOVE LEFT An oblique aerial view of the destruction to Hamburg's residential and business buildings south of the Stadtpark. These were among the 16,000 multi-storey buildings destroyed in the firestorm on the night of 27/28 July 1943.

LEFT Child refugees after the bombing of Hamburg in July 1943. More than a million people fled from the ruined area in the first days after the attacks. Some returned only at the end of the war.

RIGHT A British Cromwell tank guards a bridge over the River Elbe in Hamburg on 3 May 1945, a few days before the German surrender. The city still functioned as a centre of production but the areas destroyed in 1943 were only rebuilt in the postwar 1940s and 1950s.

THE FRENCH RESISTANCE

BELOW Example of the miniature wooden coffins 15 centimetres (six inches) long distributed by the Resistance to signify that a collaboratior had been singled out for retributive execution.

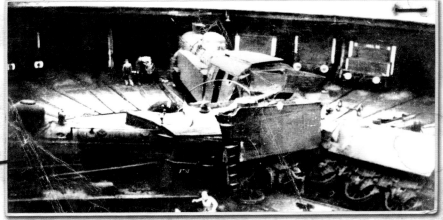

After the defeat of France the reaction of the French public to occupation was divided. There was a rallying of important sections of the population to the collaborationist Vichy regime of Marshal Pétain as a way of trying to preserve a sense of French patriotism; others tried to work with the occupiers on the assumption that this was the only realistic option; a great many, perhaps the majority, while not welcoming the consequences of defeat, tried to maintain neutrality and get on with their daily lives. A small minority, however, organized clandestine resistance from the start of the occupation and the establishment of the Vichy regime.

The resistance in France was localized. Not until 1943 were attempts made to unify the various elements under an umbrella National Council of the Resistance, but diversity remained the chief characteristic of resistance down to the liberation. The first resisters printed newspapers and leaflets, challenged or threatened collaborators, but seldom engaged in violence. Attacks on collaborators in the area of Montpellier provided the embryo of what became the "Secret Army" while the Communist resistance from 1941 organized the Francs-Tireurs et Partisans which engaged in sabotage attacks. Most resistance work consisted of collecting secret intelligence or establishing networks of sympathizers or obstructing the efforts of the German administration. Thousands of French Jews were also hidden from the Germans, an act of defiance that carried risks of heavy punishment.

The resistance was divided politically as well. Some groups were sympathetic to the exiled Charles de Gaulle and collaborated with the Free French organization based in London. They were funded and supplied by the British SOE and by MI6, which flew in agents and supplies and took back large quantities of secret intelligence information. Those groups linked with Britain also helped to organize escape routes for Allied airmen and POWs on the run,

ABOVE Wrecked railway locomotives in an engine shed at the Annemasse railway depot, destroyed by members of the French resistance.

RIGHT A poster by R Louvat from 1944 shows Allied support for the French resistance.

ABOVE Armband worn by the Free French. Featuring the cross of Lorraine and the initials of the Free French Forces of the Interior.

ABOVE An RAF Stirling bomber drops supplies by parachute to waiting French resistance fighters. Many of the canisters of weapons and equipment fell into the hands of the German or Vichy authorities, but it was an essential means to keep resistance in being.

FRENCH RESISTANCE
HELPS THROTTLE THE BOCHE

JEAN MOULIN (1899–1943)

Moulin is the most famous of the many resistance leaders who emerged in France during the German occupation. He was prefect of the Eure-et-Loir department when war broke out in 1940. He was arrested in June 1940 by the Germans for refusing to sign an affidavit blaming Senegalese soldiers for atrocities, but then released. In November 1940, the Vichy regime sacked him and he then joined the resistance, using the codename "Max". In London he met de Gaulle, who authorized him to create a united resistance organization under the title National Council of the Resistance. It was during a meeting with other resistance leaders on 21 June 1943 that he was arrested. Who denounced him is not known, but he was tortured by Klaus Barbie, refused to talk and died on the train taking him to a concentration camp, probably by committing suicide, although the story persists that he was killed by Barbie.

taking them across France and seeing them safely over the Pyrenees. Other resistance movements were based on the churches, or political movements independent of de Gaulle. The French Communists established an organization called Front National in 1941, which operated across all of France because it opposed both the Germans and the authoritarian Vichy regime.

Resistance activity increased substantially in 1943 following the German occupation of the whole of France on 11 November 1942. The Maquis groups of armed resisters were set up during 1943, many of them based in the remote mountainous regions of central and southeastern France. Their growth was helped by the German requirement for compulsory labour service in the Reich. Thousands of young French men and women, known as *réfractaires*, went into hiding to avoid labour mobilization, and although not all of them became resisters, an estimated 15–20,000 did,

joining the major resistance groups Combat, Franc-Tireur and Libération as well as a host of small local groups which sprang up during 1943 and 1944 as it became clear that German defeat was now a probability.

The impact of the resistance on the German war effort has been difficult to estimate. Much of its activity was directed towards Vichy rather than the Germans, or was targeted against French collaborators. The most significant effort came in the run-up to the Allied Normandy landings, when the resistance was nominally organized under the Free French to carry out specific acts of sabotage against railway lines and telecommunications, including the resistance actions that held up the arrival of the SS Das Reich division on its way across France to help repel the Allied invasion. As liberation approached, some Maquis groups decided on armed insurrection, but at Mont Mouchet in June 1944 and Vecors in July 1944 the German army ruthlessly suppressed them with heavy losses. Only in Savoy, with the arrival of Allied forces in southern France, did the resistance play an important part in liberating the region. During the course of the war an estimated 90,000 French resisters were killed or sent to camps under the notorious "Night and Fog" decree under which prisoners disappeared without trace. At the end of the war, however, surviving resisters played a grim part in punishing collaborators.

ENCLOSURES

1. Proclamation from the German military commander in France calling on the population not to engage in strike action against the occupying authorities, or risk severe punishment or execution. The organization of strikes or go-slows or sabotage at work was one of the many forms of resistance that the German authorities had to combat.

2. A map drawn up for the British chiefs-of-staff showing the areas where arms had been supplied to the French resistance in late 1942. The French opposition was dependent on weapons supplied by air by the British, but much of the supply ended up in the hands of the German occupiers.

MARIE-MADELEINE FOURCADE (1909–89)

Women played an important part in the French resistance, and Marie Fourcade became perhaps the most famous of them all. She began her activity from a youth centre she ran in Vichy. She went on to run the British-funded Alliance spy network after the arrest of its leader, Georges Loustaunau-Lacau. It had 3,000 informants, 429 of whom died at the hands of the German occupiers. She was arrested on 10 November 1942, but escaped to Britain, from where she continued to run the network under her codename "Hedgehog". After the war she became a leading organizer of the postwar resistance associations and was a commander of the *Légion d'Honneur*.

RIGHT A member of the resistance French Forces of the Interior hides behind a van to shelter from a German sniper at Dreux, 19 August 1944. In the last weeks of German occupation resistance forces began their own war against the occupiers.

BELOW French resistance fighters lead away a captured German soldier. In the battles to liberate French cities in the path of the advancing Allied armies German resistance rapidly crumbled. Around 10,800 collaborators were executed by the resistance in the weeks after liberation.

FROM KHARKOV TO KIEV: THE RED ARMY BREAKS THROUGH

3 SEPTEMBER 1943
Allied forces land on the mainland in southern Italy.

13 OCTOBER 1943
Italy under Marshal Badoglio declares war on Germany.

20 NOVEMBER 1943
US forces invade Betio Island on Tarawa Atoll in the South Pacific.

26–27 DECEMBER 1943
The Battle of North Cape sees the sinking of the German battlecruiser *Scharnhorst*.

ABOVE The Soviet Order of Glory. Created in November 1943 to honour those who had performed "acts of bravery in the face of the enemy".

Following the crushing victory at Kursk, Stalin ordered a general offensive along the whole Soviet-German front. The army groups that had liberated Orel and Belgorod pressed forward across the steppe and despite hasty efforts to reinforce the German 2nd Corps at Kharkov, the speed of the Soviet advance created the danger of encirclement and General Raus withdrew his forces on 22 August, a day before the Red Army liberated a battered city.

The object was to push Axis forces back to the River Dnepr in the central Ukraine in the south, to isolate the large German forces stationed in the Crimea and to propel German Army Group Centre back from Moscow to beyond Smolensk. With no natural defensive line, von Manstein's Army Group South had to retreat at speed towards the Dnepr and cross it before the Red Army enveloped them. Over 750,000 Axis troops reached the river and crossed it by 21 September, but Soviet forces using improvised rafts and barges forced the far bank at Bukrin and Zaporozhe and established a foothold across the so-called "Panther-Wotan" defensive wall which Hitler had hoped to make his defensive rampart in the east.

The bridgehead at Zaporozhe was used as the springboard for the Soviet army groups South and Southwest, under General Tolbukhin and General Malinovsky, to launch a major assault to cut off the 650,000 troops of Field Marshal von Kleist's Army Group A who had retreated to the Crimea from the Caucasus earlier in the year. By 1 December, the Red Army had reached Kherson and had bypassed the Crimean peninsula, cutting off the German garrison and approaching the town of Odessa. General Ivan Konev's Steppe Army Group captured

ABOVE Soviet forces on the outskirts of the ruined city of Kharkov which was captured by the Soviet 69th Army on 23 August 1943, the fourth time the city had changed hands in the course of the war.

RIGHT THE PPS43 submachine gun used by Soviet forces in the latter part of the war.

BELOW Red Army soldiers man an anti-aircraft gun in a square in Kharkov during the campaign for the city in February 1943. The German counter-offensive in March 1943 completed the destruction of Russia's fourth-largest city. When the city was liberated in August 1943 in Operation "Rumiantsev" there was little but rubble left.

MARSHAL RODION MALINOVSKY (1898–1967)

Malinovsky was one of that remarkable cohort of senior Soviet commanders who rose from the humble rank of private in the First World War to become a marshal in the Second. The son of peasants in Odessa, he ran away to join the army in 1914 at the age of 15, was decorated for bravery and sent to France as part of the Russian Expeditionary Force. He returned to Russia in 1919 and fought for the new Red Army in the Civil War. He became a regular soldier and volunteered for service in Spain in 1936 to help the Republic. He survived Stalin's purges, unlike many of those who went to Spain, and in 1941 was commanding a rifle corps in his home town, Odessa. He fought in all the major campaigns in the south, and held off von Manstein's efforts to relieve Paulus in Stalingrad. As commander of the 3rd Ukrainian Front (and later the 2nd Ukrainian Front), he cleared the Axis from southern Russia, pushed into Hungary and captured Vienna in April 1945. He succeeded Zhukov as defence minister in 1957 and played a leading part in the Cuban missile crisis in 1962.

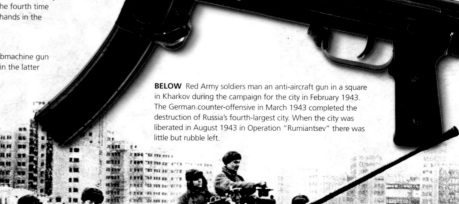

Cherkassy to the north and prepared to cross the river towards Korsun and Kirovograd. Although tank and air strength were not dissimilar, the Red Army had twice as many men in the field and four times as much artillery. Red Army soldiers had all the moral advantages of victory that German armies had possessed two years before; after Kursk there was no doubt that German forces were fighting a desperate war of defence, while Soviet soldiers were fighting to liberate their homeland.

Further to the north, two Soviet army groups attacked Army Group Centre and pushed it back beyond Smolensk, which was liberated on 25 September. The key prize was the Ukrainian capital of Kiev, which had been the scene of a humiliating encirclement for the Red Army in the late summer of 1941. Two Soviet fronts, Vatutin's Voronezh Army Group and Rokossovsky's Centre Army Group, pushed forward towards the Dnepr on either side of Kiev, establishing many small bridgeheads (a total of 40 by 25 September), which were subject to fierce German counter-attack. One small bridgehead was neglected in the swampy land around the village of Liutezh, and Vatutin, his army group now renamed 1st Ukrainian, was ordered to send men and armour into the small enclave undetected as the stepping-off point for an assault on Kiev. During late October, the 3rd Guards Tank Corps was moved into the marshland in complete secrecy.

RIGHT The German Field Marshal Erich von Manstein who organized the German retreat from Kursk in August 1943 examining operations maps with his staff. On 28 August he warned Hitler that German Army Group South could no longer hold the southern Ukraine.

RIGHT German dead from a Waffen-SS unit, the armed wing of the SS organization, which numbered around 800,000 by 1944. The SS units were, in general, better armed, and gained a reputation for greater brutality in battle.

BELOW German forces retreating in late 1943 across the last usable bridge over the Dnepr River. The remaining bridges had been blown by German engineers but Red Army soldiers improvised crossings on primitive rafts and boats.

Von Manstein expected a Soviet attack from the dry bridgeheads to the south of the city, but on 3 November two armies attacked out of the swamps to the north. By 6 November, the Red Army had entered the city and it was secured on the following day after bitter fighting. Vatutin ordered his forces to push on and by the end of December 1943 they were 160 kilometres (100 miles) beyond Kiev. Losses during the seizure of the city were remarkably low by the standards of fighting on the Eastern Front – a total of 6,491 dead or captured – but the subsequent defence of the city cost a further 26,000. In only a few months, Axis forces had been cleared from almost two-thirds of the territory they had occupied at the limit of their advance. In Moscow the capture of Kiev was celebrated with a magnificent fireworks display. At the celebration of the Revolution on 7 November, Stalin spoke of "the year of the great turning point".

ILYA EHRENBURG (1891–1967)

A Russian writer, poet and journalist, Ehrenburg is best remembered for his wartime propaganda urging Red Army soldiers to hate the Germans. He was a supporter of the Revolution when it came, but his sympathies were with the Menshevik Social Democrats rather than with Lenin's Bolsheviks. He left Russia to live in Paris but returned to Stalin's Soviet Union in 1939 where he was recruited to write poems and articles for the Red Army journals. In 1942 he wrote, "If you have killed one German, kill another. There is nothing jollier than German corpses." After the war he edited with Vasily Grossman the *Black Book of Russian Jewry*, harrowing accounts of the Holocaust in Russia, but the regime suppressed it.

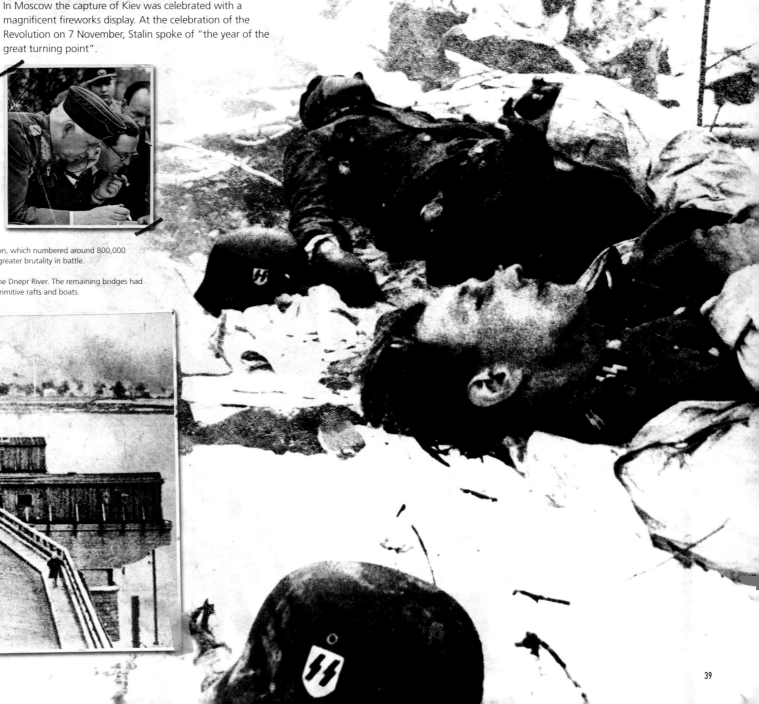

ITALY: INVASION AND SURRENDER

ABOVE Badge of the British 8th Army.

ABOVE The forward 380-millimetre (15-inch) guns of the British battleship HMS *Warspite* bombarding the Italian coast at Reggio during the early stages of the Allied landings on the mainland of southern Italy. Naval power played an important part in supporting ground operations in the Italian campaign.

ABOVE British troops and vehicles of the 8th Army's 46th Division unload on the beach at Salerno, 9 September 1943. After meeting light resistance at first, the bridgehead came under heavy attack.

LEFT Amphibious DUKWs, known as "ducks", enter the water at Messina in Sicily to cross the narrow straits to mainland Italy on 3 September 1943 during Operation "Baytown".

The decision to invade Italy after the conquest of Sicily in August 1943 was accelerated by the fall of Mussolini's regime on 25 July. The Allies hoped to be able to capitalize on the change in government to take Italy out of the war before the Germans could reinforce the peninsula adequately. Negotiations with the new regime of Marshal Badoglio were slow to produce a result. On 3 September the Italian armistice was signed at Cassibile, but by that point the Germans had succeeded in strengthening their forces in Italy from six to 18 divisions. It was essential for German strategy that the Allies should be kept as far south as possible, to avoid the establishment of airfields for the bombing of southern Germany and to make it impossible to use Italy as a military roadway into German-occupied Europe.

By the time the armistice was formally announced on 8 September, the Allies had already begun to move onto the Italian mainland. The plan was to land substantial forces in the Gulf of Salerno, south of Naples, and then to move northwards rapidly to take Naples and Rome and south to

take over the Italian "heel and toe". Lieutenant General Mark Clark was put in command of the US 5th Army, consisting of the US 6th Corps and the British 10th Corps, which would land on either side of the River Sele which flowed into the gulf. Before this operation, Montgomery took part of the 8th Army across the Straits of Messina to land unopposed on the morning of 3 September, shortly before the armistice came into effect. The 8th Army then began to push up through Calabria with the eventual aim of meeting up with the forces sent ashore at Salerno.

The situation in Italy was chaotic following the declaration of the armistice; Badoglio, the king and the General Staff fled south to join the Allies, leaving no orders for the large Italian army. German forces immediately disarmed Italian soldiers, but in some cases they resisted, only to be brutally treated and shot out of hand. Some 650,000 Italian soldiers were sent as POWs to Germany, where they became forced labourers. The Italian fleet fled to Malta, but was hit by the German air force with new remote-controlled bombs and

GENERAL MARK CLARK (1896–1984)

One of the best-known American generals in the Second World War, Clark rose rapidly from the rank of major in the 1930s to become, by mid-1942, chief-of-staff of US Army Ground Forces with the strong backing of his mentor, General George Marshall. In October 1942, he was made deputy commander-in-chief of Allied forces in North Africa, and went on to lead the US 5th Army for the invasion of Italy in September 1943 as the youngest lieutenant general in the army. Though he was often criticized for his handling of operations in Italy, including the decision to bombard the historic monastery at Monte Cassino, he became commander-in-chief of all Allied ground forces in Italy in December 1944 and by the end of the war was commander of all Allied forces in Italy. In 1949, he became chief of army field forces and commanded the United Nations forces in the Korean War, signing the ceasefire with North Korea in 1953.

the battleship *Roma* was sunk. The country was divided in two, the far south governed by Badoglio together with the Allies, the north by a new Fascist Italian Social Republic, based in the town of Salò on the shores of Lake Garda, with Mussolini as its nominal leader but the German authorities under Field Marshal Kesselring the real rulers.

On 9 September, Clark's task force sailed for Salerno, already aware that the landing would be strongly resisted by the German occupiers. A fleet of 627 ships arrived off the coast and the naval vessels subjected the coastal area to a fierce bombardment. The British forces under Lieutenant General McCreery landed to the north of the Gulf of Salerno and the Americans under Major General Dawley in the south; although small bridgeheads were secured, shortages of air support and the stiff resistance of the Panzer divisions

assigned to the German defence led to a dangerous situation by 12 September, as General von Vietinghoff's growing force began a powerful counter-offensive.

The Allies began to plan for evacuation, but the 82nd US Airborne Division was dropped into the danger zone, while aircraft and extra naval vessels were drafted in to bombard the enemy, and by 16 September German forces began to pull back. By 20 September, the rest of the 8th Army, making its way against much lighter opposition from Taranto and Bari, established firm contact with the Salerno beachhead. The German force pulled back to a prepared line north of Naples, and the port was occupied by Allied forces on 1 October. The scene was now set for a long and bitter campaign through difficult mountain country along the whole length of the Italian peninsula.

ABOVE Spitfire fighters with American pilots lined up on a former German airfield near Salerno on 3 October 1943. The wreckage of German aircraft and equipment was caused by heavy attacks by the Allied Mediterranean Strategic Air Forces.

COLONEL GENERAL HEINRICH VON VIETINGHOFF (1887–1952)

A career soldier from an aristocratic military family, von Vietinghoff served in the First World War as a junior officer on the General Staff, and by 1936 was a major general in command of a Panzer corps. In August 1943, he was sent to command the 10th Army in Italy, which he did until January 1945, when he was posted briefly as commander of the army group defending Courland against the Red Army. He acted as deputy for Kesselring as commander-in-chief southwest from October 1944 to January 1945, and was then made full commander-in-chief from 15 March 1945 until 29 April, when he surrendered his forces to the Allies. After the war, he was one of a group of experts recruited by Chancellor Adenauer who recommended German inclusion in a Western European defence system.

ENCLOSURES

1. An exchange of telegrams in August 1943 over the proposal to make Rome an open city and prevent the bombing of its valuable architecture and archaeological sites. The attempt to protect the city failed. The first attack had already taken place on 19 July 1943 and a further 50 operations were carried out, resulting in 7,000 Italian casualties.

2. The front page of the Eighth Army News on 3 September 1943 announces the invasion of mainland Italy. As British forces crossed into Calabria in the "toe" of Italy, the Italian government of Marshal Badoglio sought an armistice from the Allies. Five days later Italy's surrender was announced.

ABOVE German anti-tank unit in combat with Allied forces on the perimeter around the Salerno bridgehead. German forces almost succeeded in forcing the Allies to evacuate.

RIGHT The official signing at the Advanced Allied Headquarters, Sicily, of the Italian Armistice, on 3 September 1943. Left to right: Mr Montenari Italian Foreign Office, General W B Smith, American Chief of Staff, and General G Castellano, Chief of Staff to General Ambrosio, signing the terms of the armistice.

OPERATION "CARTWHEEL": WAR FOR NEW GUINEA

Following the defeat of the Japanese on Guadalcanal in February 1943, the Japanese naval and military leaders planned to strengthen their presence on New Guinea and to hold a defensive line from there through the northern Solomons to the Gilbert and Marshall islands. During the first three months of 1943, Lieutenant General Hatazo Adachi's 18th Army was transferred to the eastern coast of New Guinea and a large air component, the 4th Air Army, was based at Wewak, far enough from the American and Australian air forces in the southern tip of the island to avoid direct attack. The object was to move back down the island to capture Port Moresby, the target for Japanese ambitions a year before.

General MacArthur planned to consolidate the victory at Guadalcanal, which had demonstrated the growing superiority of American naval power in the southwest Pacific, by launching a major operation, codenamed "Cartwheel", against the main Japanese base at Rabaul on New Britain and the Japanese forces in northern New Guinea. On New Guinea itself an Australian army group, the New Guinea Force, with five Australian divisions and one American, was assigned to attack the Japanese based at Lae and Salamaua. The all-American Alamo Force, backed by a powerful naval and air component, was to neutralize Rabaul and attack New Britain and the Admiralty Islands, further to the north.

The Japanese attacked first in an attempt to seize the Allied airstrip at Wau but they were beaten off in bitter

ABOVE A Beaufort Bomber of No. 8 Squadron Royal Australian Air Force above the shoreline during a bombing attack on Wewak, the site of the largest Japanese airbase on mainland New Guinea.

ABOVE A Japanese national flag, given to Japanese soldiers by friends and family and carried to encourage personal good luck and patriotic virtue. They were inscribed with messages of good fortune and slogans of victory and honour to the emperor.

BELOW United states troops rush ashore during the landing at Saidor on the northern coast of New Guinea, 2 January 1944. This was part of the coast-hopping operations designed to outflank the Japanese defenders during Operation Cartwheel.

THE BATTLE OF THE BISMARCK SEA

On 23 February 1943, 7,000 men of the Japanese 51st Division embarked in eight transport vessels at the main Japanese base at Rabaul in the northern Solomon Islands, bound for northern New Guinea. They were escorted by eight destroyers. American forces had been warned in advance of the convoy through Pacific ULTRA intelligence and on 2 March began a series of attacks by day and night as the boats crossed the Bismarck Sea. All the transport vessels were sunk and four of the destroyers, with the loss of 3,664 of the division. The Japanese commander in New Guinea, Lieutenant General Hatazo Adachi, was among the 950 survivors to reach the Japanese base at Lae.

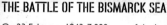

XXXXX 8 IMAMURA
Emirau Is.
Admiralty Islands
29 Feb.
Manus Is.
20 Mar.
Kavieng
PACIFIC OCEAN
Wewak
XXXX SE FLEET KUSAKA
Bismarck Archipelago
Bogia
New Ireland
Alexishafen
26 Apr.
Bismarck Sea
26 Dec.
Rabaul
Green Is. **15 Feb.**
XXXX 18 ADACHI
Madang
Saidor
Talasea
New Britain
Bougainville
XXXXX SOUTH PACIFIC AREA HALSEY
15 Dec.
Gasmata
Torokina
XXXX 8 FLEET MIKAWA
1 Nov.
Choiseul
27–28 Oct.
Lae
12 Sep.
Wau
Salamaua
Morobe
Shortlands
Treasury Is.
Santa Isabel
The Slot
PAPUA
Buna
Solomon Sea
27 Oct.
New Georgia
Owen Stanley Range
Kokoda
Goodenough Is.
Woodlark Is.
Russell Is.
Malaita
Gulf of Papua
30 Jun.–27 Aug.
Henderson Field
Port Moresby
Abau
Guadalcanal
XXXXX SOUTHWEST PACIFIC AREA MACARTHUR
Milne Bay
Louisiade Archipelago
San Cristobal
Coral Sea

Operation "Cartwheel", June 1943–April 1944 | Japanese Operation "I-Go" airstrikes, April 1943 | US and British Commonwealth advances | ✕ Naval battles

fighting. Then, on 29 June, the Allied attack began on the Japanese bases at Lae and Salamaua. To speed up the advance, Lieutenant General Kenney's US 5th Air Force built a secret airfield closer to the Japanese air base at Wewak from which he launched two devastating attacks on 17 and 18 August, leaving the Japanese with just 38 serviceable aircraft. The Japanese army defended to the death, and not until 16 September did the Australians overrun Lae and Salamaua and another three months were needed before the whole of the Huon Peninsula was in Allied hands.

While this first campaign was completed, US forces landed on western New Britain on 15 December. The previous month, strong carrier forces had neutralized any threat from the Japanese base at Rabaul, while the main concentration of the Japanese fleet, at the island of Truk in the Carolines group further north, was too weak to contest every avenue of American advance. After landings in the Admiralty Islands between 29 February and 20 March 1944, the American Fast Carrier Force commanded by Vice Admiral

Marc Mitscher swung round to mount operations on the northern coast of New Guinea far behind Adachi's retreating 18th Army, cutting off his avenue of escape. Strong forces were landed at Hollandia on 30 March and Aitape on 22 April. Adachi ordered his force to attack the US perimeter in July 1944, but was beaten back. He retreated with what was left of his force into the high mountains inland, and played no further part in the war.

Operation "Cartwheel" confirmed that the balance of power had swung firmly in favour of the Allies in the southwest Pacific. Although the Japanese had held the long frontier of their conquered Pacific empire for two years, it was only because fighting in the tough tropical conditions of the region was a slow process, while Japanese forces resisted with almost complete disregard for their losses and in spite of debilitating diseases and persistent hunger. The refusal to give up lent the fighting a brutal character which Allied forces did not encounter in the Mediterranean or Western Europe.

BELOW Australian soldiers crossing the Faria River in the Faria valley in New Guinea on their way back to base. Australian forces played a major part in the fight against the Japanese on the island.

LIEUTENANT GENERAL HATAZO ADACHI (1884–1947)

Hatazo Adachi had a reputation for leading his men from the front, even when he reached the rank of general. The son of a poor samurai family, he joined the Japanese army and began service with the 1st Imperial Guards Division. He served in Manchuria in 1933, and then as a colonel in the Sino-Japanese war, where he was wounded by mortar fire. In 1941–42 he was chief-of-staff of the North China Area Army responsible for hunting down Chinese Communists. In November 1942, he was posted to Rabaul to take command of the 18th Army for the campaign on New Guinea. In 1944, his forces were isolated on the island, and were decimated by malaria and hunger. In September 1945, he surrendered and was charged with war crimes by the Australian government. Sentenced to life imprisonment, he committed ritual suicide with a paring knife on 10 September 1947.

ABOVE An American unit on the Soputa front, near the New Guinea port of Buna, carrying wounded comrades back to headquarters after 11 days' continuous combat during the campaign to drive Japanese forces out of the southern areas of the island.

BELOW The Japanese commander on New Guinea, Lieutenant General Hatazo Adachi, arrives on 13 September 1945 at Cape Wom airbase, Wewak, for the formal surrender of his few remaining forces.

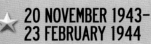
ISLAND-HOPPING IN THE PACIFIC: GILBERT AND MARSHALL ISLANDS

22–26 NOVEMBER 1943
Cairo Conference of Churchill, Roosevelt and Chiang Kaishek discusses strategy for the Far East.

28 DECEMBER 1943
Italian city of Ortona is captured after bitter fighting along the Gustav Line.

4 JANUARY 1944
Red Army crosses the pre-1939 Polish border into German-occupied Europe.

27 JANUARY 1944
The Siege of Leningrad is finally lifted after the death of an estimated one million inhabitants.

15 FEBRUARY 1944
The monastery of Monte Cassino is heavily bombed by the Allies and completely destroyed.

17 FEBRUARY 1944
Capture of "Cherkassy Pocket" by Konev's forces leaves 19,000 Germans dead or captured.

The assault on New Guinea and Rabaul in the second half of 1943 was one wing of a two-pronged campaign. A second line of attack was launched through the Solomon Islands north of Guadalcanal and on into the central Pacific against the outlying Gilbert and Marshall islands, viewed as stepping-stones to the distant Marianas, which were within striking distance of Japan for the US Army Air Force's new generation of long-range heavy bombers, the B-29 Superfortress.

ABOVE United States marines from the 2nd Marine Division wade through shallow water in the invasion of Makin Atoll. The US commanders had little knowledge of Japanese strength on the island, but in this case the small garrison of 800 was overcome in three days of fighting which proved less costly than on neighbouring Tarawa.

LEFT An American cruiser fires at Japanese positions on Makin Atoll, 20 November 1943, during an operation in the Gilbert Islands, northeast of the Solomons.

In June 1943, Admiral William Halsey's Third Fleet began the task of capturing the main islands of the southern Solomons. Rendova Island was taken on 30 June, then New Georgia was attacked and the base at Munda captured on 4–5 August. Japanese convoys sent to help the endangered garrisons were destroyed in two battles in the Kula Gulf and the Vella Gulf, and on 1 November US forces, supported by the 3rd New Zealand Division, landed on the main island of Bougainville, where air bases could be set up to bomb the Japanese base at Rabaul. Japanese reinforcements were hastily sent to the island, where the Japanese garrison numbered around 40,000 men, but Halsey was able to call on extensive air support to contain the Japanese threat while an assault by two of his carriers on the powerful fleet of Vice Admiral Kurita at Rabaul forced a Japanese withdrawal. The Japanese were bottled up on Bougainville for the rest of the war, at the end of which 23,000 finally surrendered.

Further north, Admiral Nimitz prepared to assault the Gilbert and Marshall islands. A force of 200 ships was assembled, with 35,000 soldiers and 6,000 vehicles. On 13 November, a sustained naval bombardment began against the Makin and Tarawa atolls in the Gilbert

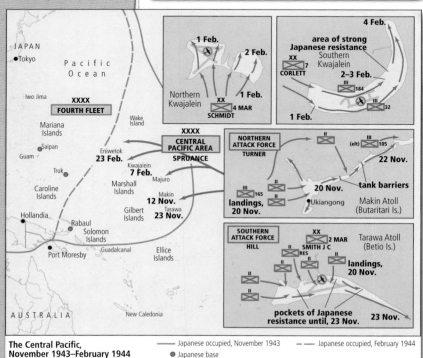

The Central Pacific, November 1943–February 1944

— Japanese occupied, November 1943   -- Japanese occupied, February 1944
● Japanese base

THE BATTLE FOR TARAWA

The battle for the small island of Betio on the edge of Tarawa atoll in the Gilbert Islands was one of the toughest battles of the Pacific War. Only 4,500 Japanese marines garrisoned the island, but they were well supplied and dug in to deep defensive positions, including 500 pillboxes and a network of concealed trenches. The US naval force that mounted the operation included no fewer than 17 aircraft carriers and 12 battleships and transported 35,000 US marines and soldiers. They attacked on 20 November 1943, but intense Japanese fire and difficult tidal waters pinned the invaders on the beaches. There followed three days of fierce fighting, but vastly superior manpower and supplies gradually allowed the American forces to gain the upper hand. At the end of the battle, only 17 Japanese soldiers were left alive, but a total of 990 US marines and 687 sailors lost their lives, a level of casualties that prompted strong criticism of the operation among the American public.

ABOVE US Marines clear a Japanese pillbox on the Tarawa atoll.

REAR ADMIRAL MARC A MITSCHER (1887-1947)

One of the pioneers of naval aviation in the US Navy, Marc Mitscher played an important part in driving the Japanese from the central Pacific during the Second World War. He joined the navy in 1906, transferring to the Aeronautics Section in 1915. He was one of three navy pilots who flew across the Atlantic in flying boats in 1919. He was assistant chief of the Bureau of Aeronautics from 1939 to 1941, and then took command of the aircraft carrier USS *Hornet* from which the Doolittle raid was launched against Japanese cities in April 1942. His carrier saw action at Midway, and in April 1943 he became air commander in the Solomons. He was appointed to command carrier Task Force 58 (later known as the Fast Carrier Task Force) which harried the Japanese in New Guinea and the Marianas and in March 1944 was promoted to vice admiral. At the end of the war he was appointed deputy chief of naval operations responsible for aviation, and in 1946 became commander-in-chief of the Atlantic Fleet.

ABOVE A US marine prepares to throw a hand grenade during the invasion of the tiny Betio Island on the southern shore of the lagoon formed by Tarawa Atoll. The fighting for Betio was among the fiercest and most costly of the island campaign.

LEFT Dead Japanese soldiers, who shot themselves rather surrender to the Americans, on Namur Island.

ENCLOSURES

1. A series of urgent messages sent by United States marines in the assault on Tarawa Atoll between 20 and 23 November 1943. The landing was strongly opposed by Japanese troops dug into hidden positions and the marines were pinned down on the beach for two days before US firepower succeeded in driving the Japanese garrison back.
2. The action report of 10 December 1943 from Admiral Raymond Spruance detailing the role of his Central Pacific Area fleet in the 'island-hopping' campaigns of November and December 1943. His carriers played a critical role in supplying air support for the brief island campaigns.
3. A narrative account from one US marine to another of the battle to secure Tarawa between 21 and 29 November 1943. Although the main base on Betio island was secured by 23 November the many outlying islands of the atoll still had to be cleared of pockets of Japanese resistance, where Japanese soldiers fought until they were killed.

LEFT A US naval rating playing the trumpet in an informal entertainment for the troops on Tarawa Atoll on New Year's Eve 1943, five weeks after its capture.

Islands. The attack, codenamed Operation "Galvanic", began on 20 November against Makin Atoll, which was secured by 23 November after limited but fierce fighting by a small Japanese garrison of 800 soldiers, which had no aircraft and was commanded by no one more senior than a first lieutenant. A Japanese submarine from Truk sank a US escort carrier, *Liscombe Bay*. Betio Island on Tarawa Atoll took the same time to secure, but only after bitter and costly fighting for both sides. Attention then shifted to the Marshall Islands further north, a German colony taken over as a mandate by the Japanese in 1919. The objective here was to capture the main Japanese base on Kwajalein Atoll in an operation codenamed "Flintlock". Rear Admiral Charles Pownall's Task Force 50 bombarded the Japanese positions more than a month before the assault took place, followed by heavy attacks from land-based aircraft.

On 1 February, an armada of 297 ships brought the US 7th Infantry Division to Kwajalein, while the 4th Marine Division went on to the Roi and Namur islands further to the north of the group. In total 84,000 troops were involved in

the hope of avoiding the costly battles experienced in the Gilberts. After six days of heavy fighting, all three islands were secure; on Kwajalein only 265 Japanese soldiers were taken alive out of a garrison of 4,000. Nimitz then ordered a further operation against the Engei and Eniwotek atolls, 560 kilometres (350 miles) northwest of Kwajalein. Attacks here secured the islands between 17 and 23 February. The US naval forces were now within striking distance of the Marianas, and aircraft from the Marshalls could attack the main Japanese naval base at Truk. Although there was much argument over the merits of the island-hopping campaign, where tiny atolls were secured at a high cost in casualties, Nimitz was keen to push the central Pacific avenue to Japan as a more efficient, faster and ultimately less costly strategy than MacArthur's idea of attacking through the East Indies and the Philippines against heavy Japanese force concentrations. The result was a division of resources between two different campaigns, and a growing sense of rivalry between the army and navy over who would defeat Japan first.

BELOW A US soldier uses a jeep with a billboard on the back to direct bombers to their parking places on the Eniwetok airstrip captured from the Japanese in the Marshall Islands on 23 February 1944. In the background can be seen B-24 Liberator bombers.

FOLLOW ME

THE BIG THREE: THE TEHERAN CONFERENCE

10 OCTOBER 1943
Foreign Ministers' Conference at Moscow prepares ground for Teheran.

18 NOVEMBER 1943
Start of major bombing campaign by RAF Bomber Command against the German capital.

28 NOVEMBER 1943
US Forces complete the conquest of Tarawa Atoll in the South Pacific.

2 DECEMBER 1943
German air force attacks the Italian port of Bari causing a massive explosion of Allied ammunition stores.

In November 1943, the three leaders of the major Allied powers met together for the first time in the Iranian capital, Teheran. The conference, codenamed "Eureka", was called to resolve major issues of Allied strategy for the last phase of the war, but Roosevelt hoped that it might lay the foundation for a close personal relationship with Stalin as the basis for a postwar political settlement.

Teheran was not the first choice for the summit venue. Roosevelt had suggested the Bering Straits, Khartoum, Cairo and Asmara in Somaliland, but Stalin insisted that he wanted to stay in touch with developments on the fighting front (Kiev was finally liberated three weeks before the conference). Roosevelt had to travel 11,250 kilometres (7,000 miles) to get to Teheran, Churchill some 6,500 kilometres (4,000 miles). On the way to Teheran, they halted at Cairo, where a preliminary conference was held with China's Nationalist leader, Chiang Kaishek, from 23 to 26 November. Stalin had been invited to this meeting, codenamed "Sextant", but he refused since the Soviet Union was not yet at war with Japan. "Sextant" was the occasion to reiterate Western Allied support for the Chinese struggle. The Cairo Declaration issued at the end of the conference committed the Allies to confiscating all Japan's imperial territories, returning Chinese territory to China and creating an independent Korea.

ABOVE Allied political and military leaders meeting in Cairo before the conference in Teheran. The first conference, codenamed "Sextant", took place from 23 to 26 November 1943 and involved Churchill, Roosevelt and the Chinese leader Chiang Kaishek (seated left).

BELOW Soviet Marshal Kliment Voroshilov shows the "Sword of Stalingrad" to President Roosevelt during an informal meeting in Teheran. The sword was a gift to the Soviet people from the British monarch, King George VI, and was presented on his behalf by Churchill on 28 November 1943.

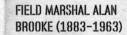

FIELD MARSHAL ALAN BROOKE (1883–1963)

Chief of the Imperial General Staff from 1941 to 1946, Alan Brooke played a central role in Britain's war effort, and acted throughout the war as a brake on Churchill's more impetuous strategic ideas. An Ulsterman by birth, he joined the Royal Artillery before 1914 and fought as an artilleryman during the First World War, rising from the rank of lieutenant to lieutenant colonel by 1918. He was an officer of outstanding talent, becoming a major general in 1935, and a lieutenant general three years later as Commander of the Anti-Aircraft Command. He led the British 2nd Corps in the Battle of France, and after his return to England was made Commander-in-Chief Home Forces. In December 1941, he was promoted to Chief of the Imperial General Staff, and became the senior advisor to the government. He was a permanent member of the combined chiefs-of-staff and negotiated firmly with his American counterparts, who respected his sharp intellect and power of speech, though he was not much liked by them. In 1944, he was created a field marshal, and in 1946 was made a viscount. After the war, he became a director of the Midland Bank and chancellor of Queen's University, Belfast.

In Teheran, formally within the British sphere in Iran, there was extravagant security, including a regiment of Indian Sikhs to protect Churchill, who stayed at the British Embassy. On the pretext that there was a risk to Roosevelt's safety, the president was persuaded to stay in a house in the grounds of the Soviet Embassy. This symbolized the pattern of the conference, in which Roosevelt sought to make common cause with Stalin and Churchill was left isolated by the two senior partners in the so-called Grand Alliance. Stalin wanted a commitment from the West for a second front in France, which Roosevelt and his military advisers were keen to promise, but Churchill wanted to use the conference as a further opportunity to press his preferred strategy of an attack from the Mediterranean on the "soft underbelly" of German-occupied Europe which had now been exposed by the surrender of Italy.

These arguments were played out in the first two days of negotiations. On the second day, Roosevelt promised a second front in May 1944 and Churchill was forced to comply even though he and his senior advisers, including the chief of the Imperial General Staff, General Alan Brooke, thought the risk of a major cross-Channel invasion very high. A diversionary attack on southern France was also promised (Operation "Anvil") and approved by Stalin, although once again Churchill was strongly sceptical of its value. The Soviet side offered to mount a powerful offensive to coincide with the invasion in the west, and Stalin also pledged the

ABOVE Sergeant Kipral Singh of the 3rd Battalion, 11th Sikh Regimment, handing a birthday gift to Churchill. The Sikh Regiment formed Churchill's guard at Teheran.

ABOVE Stalin raises his glass in a toast to Churchill at a reception held at the British Embassy on 30 November 1943 during the Teheran Conference. The British foreign secretary, Anthony Eden, stands on Churchill's right.

LEFT Roosevelt, Churchill and Stalin (left to right) at the British Embassy in Teheran on the evening of 30 November 1943 to celebrate Churchill's 69th birthday. Stalin became intoxicated and by the end of the evening was exchanging toasts with the surprised embassy servants.

RIGHT Stalin (left) and Roosevelt sitting together in Teheran. They established a good rapport during the conference, much to Churchill's irritation. Roosevelt aimed to involve Stalin in a postwar international order and hoped his personal relationship would help seal Soviet-American collaboration.

Soviet Union to join the war against Japan once Germany was defeated. On the evening of 30 November, Churchill hosted a lavish dinner in honour of his birthday at the British Embassy, where Stalin taunted both Churchill and Brooke for their hostile attitude to the Soviet Union. By the end of the evening Stalin was unusually intoxicated and the sour note he had introduced was finally overcome. The following day the three leaders signed a public communiqué on the strategy agreed for the defeat of Germany.

The Teheran Conference was regarded by Roosevelt as a possible starting point for a closer political relationship between the United States and the Soviet Union which might continue into peacetime. Churchill and Roosevelt returned to Cairo to complete the "Sextant" conference between 3 and 7 December, when Roosevelt announced his decision to appoint Eisenhower as supreme commander for the invasion of France. Churchill, who had not been well for much of the Teheran Conference, went on to Morocco to convalesce.

PARTISAN WAR

In some parts of Axis-occupied Europe resistance took the form of a violent armed campaign by guerrilla fighters, or partisans as they were generally styled during the war. The main areas in which they operated were in eastern and southern Europe, in Greece, Yugoslavia, Poland, the Soviet Union and, in the last years of the war, in German-occupied northern Italy as well. In all these regions, the occupying forces often had to deploy very substantial armed forces to combat a hidden enemy committed to the armed struggle for liberation.

Partisan warfare gave the Second World War a very different character from the war of 1914–18, stemming from the deep ideological conflicts that characterized the politics of interwar and wartime Europe, but also the sense that in total war civilians were just as much part of the fighting as the soldiers. Thousands of armed civilians, some of them former soldiers, died in pitched battles with the regular troops of Germany and her allies, who treated partisan war as terrorism and responded with a savage brutality against the partisan fighters and the civilian populations among whom they hid.

The largest and militarily most significant partisan movement developed in the Soviet Union, where Stalin summoned the population, civilian and soldier, to resist by every means possible against the German enemy. Small groups formed in the forests and swamps of Belorussia and Ukraine, at first isolated and poorly armed, but from May 1942, when a central organization was set up in

Moscow, they were supplied and often led by regular Red Army men infiltrated behind the lines. Linked by radio, it became possible to co-ordinate the efforts to cut German communications and to sabotage German rear areas. German forces imposed a savage retaliation, isolating the villages suspected of activity and burning them down and murdering the inhabitants. In Belorussia, an estimated 350,000 civilians were killed alongside 30,000 partisans in the German anti-partisan sweeps. But by 1943, there were an estimated 130,000 of them and in some areas Soviet rule had been re-established. German soldiers were confined more and more to pathways across Soviet territory where it was possible to retain control through terror.

In Yugoslavia, Greece and Italy, the partisan movements were different. They were divided, usually along political lines, but, in many cases, they were also involved in a

LEFT Women fighters of the Yugoslav royalist Chetnik partisans, 17 May 1944. Women played a role in all partisan and resistance movements, both fighting and organizing supplies or hiding partisans on the run.

ABOVE LEFT German soldiers and security forces burn down a village in Belorussia. Thousands of villages were destroyed to prevent partisans from getting access to food and to punish the population in retaliation for partisan attacks.

BELOW Greek soldiers from the ELAS (National People's Liberation Army) firing on a police station in 1944 during an armed uprising in Athens. The resistance in Greece was divided on ideological grounds and gave way to civil war after the Germans left.

20–21 OCTOBER 1941
Germans murder 4,000 Yugoslavs at Kragujevac and Kraljevo in retaliation for a partisan attack.

25 NOVEMBER 1942
Greek partisans destroy the Gorgopotamos viaduct, breaking the Athens–Salonika railway.

28 SEPTEMBER 1943
Italian resisters launch insurrection in Naples before Allied liberation and 663 are killed.

1–18 OCTOBER 1943
SS division murders 1,604 Italian civilians in the village of Marzabotto, including 150 children.

20 OCTOBER 1944
Yugoslav capital Belgrade recaptured by Tito's partisan army.

ABOVE German anti-partisan pin, awarded to those fighting groups of partisans in occupied Europe.

TITO (JOSIP BROZ) (1892–1980)

Born of mixed Croat and Slovene parentage, Broz became a metal-worker and an active socialist. Imprisoned in 1914 for anti-war activities, he was then sent to the Russian front and captured in 1915. During the Russian Revolution he joined the Red Army, but eventually made his way back to Yugoslavia in 1920. There he became an active Communist, adopting the cover name Tito in 1934, and eventually general secretary of the Yugoslav Communist Party in 1937. In 1941, after the German invasion, he was declared military commander of the Communist resistance and was the most prominent figure on the Anti-Fascist Council. In 1944–45, Tito's movement liberated much of Yugoslavia, and in March 1945 he headed the Yugoslav provisional government. He was elected prime minister in November 1945 and was president from 1953 until his death in 1980.

PANTELEYEMON PONOMARENKO (1902–84)

The leader of the Soviet partisan movement appointed by Stalin on 30 May 1942 to head the Central Staff for Partisan Warfare, Ponomarenko acted as the chief-of staff of the guerrilla movement. He was a Red Army general and a senior party official, appointed in 1938 after the purges as first secretary of the Belorussian Communist Party. He played a part in "cleansing" the areas of Belorussia seized from Poland in 1939 of bourgeois and counter-revolutionary elements. He then helped to organize partisan resistance in the area after the German invasion before being summoned to Moscow. After the war, he was a member of the Politburo in 1952–53 and ambassador to Poland from 1955 to 1957. He was the co-founder of the Soviet National Jazz Orchestra based in the Belorussian capital, Minsk.

BELOW Ponomarenko (far left) in October 1939, in his role as Secretary of the Belorussian Communist Party at the Presidium of the First Conference of the People's Representatives of Western Belorussia.

political struggle against the old order, so that they targeted collaborators or prewar political enemies as much as the Axis enemy. In Yugoslavia a pro-monarchist Serb movement under General Draža Mihailovic fought against the Yugoslav Communist resistance led by Tito, and seldom confronted the Germans. Tito's movement was almost annihilated in 1941–42 but by the end of 1943 around 200,000 fighters had been organized, helped by the British, who decided that Tito's forces were the most likely to offer them serious military help. An estimated 1.2 million died in the conflicts in Yugoslavia from racial and political vendettas as well as Axis anti-partisan sweeps.

In Greece and Italy, the principal partisan groups were Communists. The Greek National People's Liberation Army (ELAS) and its political wing, the National Liberation Front (EAM), fought the Germans and the non-Communist National Republican Greek League. A truce was agreed in 1944 but EAM was the strongest organization, succeeding in controlling parts of rural Greece by 1944 when the Germans withdrew. Partisan war against the Germans was then followed by partisan war against the returning Greek government and its British allies, which developed into the Greek Civil War. In Italy the partisan movement emerged as a response to the harsh German occupation following Italian surrender in September 1943. A Committee for National Liberation was established, dominated by Communists, but there were also other partisan groups, including Justice and Liberty, representing the non-Communist Party of Action. An estimated 100,000 joined by 1944, based in the mountain areas of central and northern Italy, but fierce German retaliation, assisted by regiments of anti-Communist

Cossacks recruited from Russia, brought the Italian partisan movement to a point of crisis by early 1945.

Everywhere the Germans faced partisan activity they reacted with ferocity against what they regarded as an illegitimate form of warfare. In Italy, 40,000 died in retaliation raids and anti-partisan operations, including 560 men, women and children butchered by the SS 16th Panzer Division at the village of Sant'Anna di Stazzema in August 1944. In Slovakia, 25,000 were killed after an anti-German rising in August 1944 organized by Slovak partisans and a number of regular soldiers. Partisan activity often failed to dent the German war effort, but it gave the German army, frustrated and in retreat, a weaker enemy on whom they could vent their fury.

ABOVE A Serbian partisan hangs from a lampost after his execution by German forces, April 1943.

ENCLOSURE
Order no. 189 issued by Stalin to the Soviet people on 5 September 1942. The order calls for a relentless partisan struggle against the German invaders and marks the beginning of a more centrally co-ordinated partisan movement which involved an estimated 300,000 by the end of the year.

ABOVE Soviet poster – "Beat the enemy mercilessly, partisans!"

RIGHT Italian partisans in action in Venice in 1945. Fierce German counter-measures in the winter of 1944–45 decimated partisan numbers, but the movement revived in the spring of 1945 as the end of the war drew near.

BATTLE OF THE NORTH CAPE

The Battle of the North Cape, fought on Boxing Day (26 December) 1943, was the last engagement fought by the Royal Navy against a major battleship. The battle had its origins in the decision by the British government in November 1943 to recommence the Arctic aid convoys to the Soviet Union, which had been suspended in March 1943 because of the threat posed by German air and sea power and shortages of naval shipping. The two large German ships in Norwegian waters, the battleship *Tirpitz* and the fast battlecruiser *Scharnhorst*, had in fact done very little for most of the war and Hitler had decided that they should be scrapped. The resumption of northern convoys encouraged the German navy commander-in-chief Admiral Dönitz to order an attack so that Hitler could be shown that the large ships were not simply a waste of resources.

On 20 December, a large convoy, JW55B, left Loch Ewe in Scotland bound for the Soviet Arctic ports. An empty convoy, RA55A, was returning the other way. The two convoys would cross in the strait between Bear Island and the North Cape in northern Norway. The commander of the British Home Fleet, Admiral Fraser, suspected from intelligence evidence that the German navy would attempt to intercept the convoys, and on 23 December he took his flagship, the battleship *Duke of York*, with 360-millimetre (14-inch) guns, out to sea with a strong escort of one cruiser and four destroyers. To the east was a cruiser group under Vice Admiral Robert Burnett of *Belfast*, *Norfolk* and *Sheffield* which could also be used to defend the convoy and engage any German units.

The German commander of the *Scharnhorst*, Vice Admiral Bey, was a temporary appointment whose previous experience had been confined to destroyers. Encouraged by Dönitz to take action, the German headquarters at Kiel ordered Bey to take out his ships on Christmas Day 1943 and intercept a convoy, whose whereabouts were not known precisely, nor the position or strength of any Royal Navy force that might be protecting it. The weather

BELOW The German battlecruisers *Scharnhorst* and *Gneisenau* travel in a line with their guns firing, allegedly taken during their escape from Brest, known as the "Channel Dash" on 12 February 1942.

ABOVE The snow-covered forward gun turrets of the British cruiser HMS *Belfast* during a patrol in Arctic waters. The *Belfast* was on patrol near North Cape when the *Scharnhorst* left Norway to intercept two British convoys.

was atrocious, with heavy squally snow showers and high seas, but Bey left the safety of his fjord together with four destroyers. By the morning of 26 December, Bey had lost contact with his covering force and never regained it. Instead, the battlecruiser sailed on towards the convoy on its own, and into the path of the waiting British cruiser squadron. The *Scharnhorst* was detected by radar and then visibly and at 9.30 a.m. *Norfolk* began to engage, knocking out Bey's forward radar. The German ship made off to the north, towards the convoy.

The attack was a complete surprise for the German ship, but Bey relied on superior speed to reach the convoy ahead of the cruisers. Burnett took a shorter route and just after

VICE ADMIRAL ERICH BEY (1898–1943)

Erich Bey joined the German navy in 1916 and spent most of his subsequent career serving as an officer on destroyers. In the Norwegian campaign, as a junior captain, he commanded a four-destroyer flotilla which was among those destroyed when the Royal Navy attacked on 13 April 1940. On 10 May, he was promoted to full captain and commander of destroyers, a post he held down to his death in 1943. He was promoted to vice admiral and commanded the battleship *Scharnhorst* and a group of destroyers in the Battle of the North Cape. After the battleship was sunk he was seen badly wounded in the water, but drowned before he could be rescued.

ABOVE A painting by John Hamilton of the British battleship HMS *Duke of York* engaging the German battlecruiser *Scharnhorst* during the Battle of the North Cape.

midday contact was restored and the attack began again. This time the cruisers were damaged by the heavier shells of the battlecruiser, but Bey decided that the risk of attacking the convoy was now too great and turned for base, straight into the path of Fraser's force which was placed between the German ship and the Norwegian coast. Poor intelligence and reconnaissance left Bey in ignorance of the trap until, at 4.48 p.m., a salvo from the *Duke of York* straddled the *Scharnhorst*. The British battleship fired 52 salvos and damaged the German ship's boiler room, slowing it down to 8–10 knots. The other British ships closed in for the kill, but it took 11 torpedoes before the German ship sank at 7.45 p.m. with the loss of all but 36 of the 2,000-man crew.

The battleship *Tirpitz* stayed in Norwegian waters and, following 22 attacks by aircraft, was finally sunk on 12 November 1944 by two "Tallboy" heavy bombs with the loss of 1,204 men. Hitler's lack of confidence in battleships proved to have some foundation.

ADMIRAL BRUCE FRASER (1888–1981)

When Bruce Fraser was created a baron in 1946 he chose as his title 1st Baron Fraser of North Cape, the Arctic site where he commanded a notable Royal Navy victory in 1943. He joined the Royal Navy in 1904 and became an expert in gunnery, serving as a gunnery officer during the First World War. He fought in the intervention against the Bolshevik revolution, and briefly became a POW in 1920. In 1939, he was controller of the navy and third sea lord in the Admiralty. As commander-in-chief of the Home Fleet in 1943, he led the task force at the Battle of the North Cape. In November 1944, he was appointed commander-in-chief of the British Pacific Fleet, which took part in the invasion of Okinawa and the attacks on the Japanese home islands. He signed the Japanese Instrument of Surrender on behalf of the British forces on 2 September 1945. In 1948, he became first sea lord and chief of the Naval Staff, retiring in 1952.

ABOVE The German battleship *Tirpitz* at her berth on the Norwegian coast under air attack on 3 April 1943. Despite regular attacks from bombers the battleship remained resistant to all attempts to sink her until November 1944, though the bombing severely disabled the ship and prevented the remains of the German battle fleet fighting together.

ABOVE LEFT A scene aboard the *Scharnhorst*, one of a new generation of German fast battlecruisers with 280-millimetre (11-inch) guns which failed to fulfil the role intended for them as merchant raiders.

BELOW Blindfolded survivors of the sinking of the *Scharnhorst* are led ashore at the British naval base of Scapa Flow. Out of a crew of 2,000, only 36 survived.

THE BATTLE FOR ANZIO

ABOVE Badge of the 56th London Infantry Division.

CENTRE RIGHT (object) German anti-tank mine used against the Allies in Italy.

Following the landings at Salerno, the Allies decided on a second coastal landing a little south of Rome around the port of Anzio as a way of turning the German Gustav Line, which by late December 1943 ran from Formia on the west coast to Ortona in the east, a mainly mountainous terrain with narrow river valleys, ideal for defensive purposes. The Anzio landings, strongly supported by Churchill and organized by General Mark Clark, were designed to trap the German 10th Army, which was resisting the advance of the British 8th Army and the US-led 5th Army towards the mountain stronghold around the ancient monastery of Monte Cassino. It was also hoped that the landings would open the way for an advance to Rome.

The operation, codenamed "Shingle", carried a considerable risk because the forces involved were modest. The 6th US Army Corps under Major General John Lucas comprised the British 1st Infantry Division and the US 3rd Infantry Division, supported by commandos and rangers, and a powerful element of air support. On 22 January 1944, over 370 ships arrived off the Italian coast to be met by no initial resistance. The Allied force landed and established a narrow beachhead, but Lucas, whose immediate objectives had not been made entirely clear in the planning, dug his forces in rather than exploiting the advantage of tactical surprise. Though often criticized for the decision, it almost certainly saved the operation from disaster, for within four days Field Marshal Kesselring succeeded in improvising a six-division 14th Army under General von Mackensen, which on 1 February began a sustained assault on the perimeter of the Anzio area after a number of smaller forays.

ABOVE United States troops of the 5th Army board landing craft for the voyage to the Italian coast at Anzio where it was hoped that the Allied landing would catch German forces in a pincer movement.

Although Lucas was soon reinforced, and was strongly supported by air and sea bombardment, the German forces succeeded in containing the bridgehead in five months of bitter fighting. By mid-February, the German counter-offensive threatened to drive a salient into the Allied line, dividing the British to the north of Anzio from the Americans to the south. Probing attacks by German armoured forces pushed back British and American troops, who had begun a cautious move out from their initial defensive line. A salient formed by the British 1st Division was attacked and on 9 February the 3rd Panzer Grenadier Division recaptured Aprilia and two days later the Scots Guards were expelled from the town of Carroceto, captured on 25 January. Von Mackensen was instructed by Kesselring to concentrate

ABOVE A chaotic scene near an American medical post in the Anzio bridgehead in February 1944. After an almost unopposed landing, the fighting became fierce and losses high on both sides.

ABOVE A Sherman tank and armoured personnel carriers on the beach at Anzio on 22 January 1944. The initial landings met almost no resistance, unlike the landings at Salerno, but German forces soon regrouped and counter-attacked.

RIGHT Allied shipping unloading supplies in Anzio harbour in mid-February 1944. The bridgehead was held thanks to a regular flow of materiel and reinforcements which could be brought in by sea with a small level of risk.

his forces for a major offensive, codenamed "Fischfang" (Fish-catch) to divide the bridgehead and then expel it.

The Allies were pre-warned by ULTRA intelligence and a heavy air bombardment was directed at the German concentrations, but on 16 February von Mackensen launched a strong attack at the weak line between the British and American sectors which was only halted by a further ferocious barrage of fire from sea, air and artillery. The Germans established a salient eight kilometres (five miles) wide and three kilometres (two miles) deep but could progress no further. Six days later, Lucas was redeployed and his deputy, Major General Lucian Truscott, placed in effective command. His first action was to tour the battlefield, visiting every one of the Allied units in an effort to boost sagging morale. A second major German attack on 29 February was also repulsed. What followed was a war of attrition between the two sides: the German ring of armoured divisions was never quite powerful enough to push the bridgehead back into the sea, but the 6th Corps, despite continuous reinforcement, was too weak to break the cordon.

The trench stalemate was broken only by renewed pressure on the Gustav Line from Allied forces around Cassino. It became clear to Kesselring that the line would not hold, and German forces prepared to withdraw to defensive lines prepared further up the Italian peninsula. As the German grip weakened, Truscott prepared a fresh offensive and on 23 May Allied forces broke out of the Anzio bridgehead and drove east, intending to encircle the retreating Germans. Instead General Clark ordered a drive northwards, and Rome fell on 4 June to American forces. The costs of the Anzio campaign were high, 43,000 for the Allies, including 7,000 dead, and an estimated 40,000 for the Germans, with 5,000 killed.

ENCLOSURE

Extracts from the diary of signaller J McKay, 2 Field regiment Royal Artillery, 1st Division from the landings at Anzio in January 1944 to the Allied entry into Rome in June. The battle around Anzio came to resemble the trench warfare of the First World War until the German line crumbled in late May.

ABOVE British soldiers shelter in a trench from German shelling on 22 May 1944, shortly before the breakout from the Anzio bridgehead which opened the road to Rome.

ABOVE Two black US servicemen from the 5th Army sitting at the entrance to an air-raid shelter in March 1944 during the defence of the Anzio bridgehead. Large numbers of black Americans served in the armed forces though they were still the victims of segregation when they returned home.

RIGHT Two captured German paratroopers carrying a wounded British soldier who has lost his foot in a landmine explosion, 22 May 1944.

COLONEL GENERAL EBERHARD VON MACKENSEN (1889–1969)

A Prussian aristocrat, von Mackensen had a conventional soldier's career in the German army. He joined the army in 1908, served in the First World War where he was wounded and given a staff job, and remained in the army after 1919. By 1938, he was a major general and on the outbreak of war he was chief-of-staff of the German 14th Army. He served in France and in Army Group South in Russia, as commander of the 3rd Army Corps. In 1943, he was sent to command the 14th Army, and was retired in June 1944 after the failure to contain the Anzio bridgehead. After the war, he was tried as a war criminal and condemned to death. His sentence was commuted to 21 years in prison, but he was released in 1952.

MAJOR GENERAL JOHN LUCAS (1890–1949)

Lucas began his career in 1911 as a US cavalryman but then joined the field artillery and was wounded in service in the First World War. During the Second World War he saw service in North Africa before being selected to lead the Allied invasion of the Anzio beachhead in January 1944. He was critical of the operation and played a poor part in its execution, spending all his time as commander in an underground bunker. His relations with the British officers assigned to Anzio were strained. He was replaced in February 1944 by his deputy, Major General Truscott, and he was sent back to the United States to take command of an army.

ABOVE A photograph of the Benedictine monastery of Monte Cassino taken c.1927. The site had been a monastery since the 6th century AD and was a building of exceptional architectural and religious significance. German forces promised not to occupy the building and did not do so until it had been destroyed by Allied bombing.

The key to breaking the German grip on southcentral Italy was the heavily defended area around Cassino and the valleys of the Liri and Rapido rivers. This was the setting for one of the most bitterly contested struggles of the war in the west which led to the complete destruction of the ancient Benedictine monastery of Monte Cassino, set high on an outcrop of mountainside above the town of Cassino.

The battle for Cassino lasted five months and involved four major operations. The German 14th Panzer Corps, under General von Senger und Etterlin, bore the brunt of the defence, dug in to the rugged landscape and valley sides that made up this part of the Gustav Line. The Allied plan, set out in a directive from Alexander's headquarters on 8 November 1943, was to destroy German forces in the Liri valley and to approach Rome from the south, in conjunction with a landing at Anzio designed to roll up the German front. Early attacks in December on the German defences showed how difficult the assault would be with Allied forces that were battle-worn after the hard drive up from Sicily.

The opening battle began on 17 January 1944 when British forces tried to cross the River Garigliano and the Americans the River Rapido three days later. Small bridgeheads were secured against fierce resistance and the US 5th Army began a slow ascent towards the monastery before heavy losses forced a halt on mountains to the

ABOVE Two German paratroopers fighting in the ruins of Monte Cassino monastery during April 1944. The destroyed monastery created a natural defensive position which was abandoned only after it was clear that German forces faced the threat of possible encirclement.

Map

Germans withdraw to meet French flanking movement, 18 May

Mte. Abate
Terrelle
Mte. Belvedere
Mte. Cifalco
Rapido
Sant Elia
Mt. Cairo
Mt. Castellone
Cairo
Maiola Hill
Sant Angelo Hill
Piedimonte
Aquino
Monte Cassino
Cassino
Piumarola
Viticuso

to Rome

XXX LI MTN VON SENGER UND ETTERLIN
XXXX 14 MACKENSEN
XXX XIV
XX 44
XX 90
XX 4
XX 78
XX 8 IND
XX 1
XX 2 MOR
XX 4 MOR
XX 3 ALG
XX 71
XX 94 Mte. Maio

XXX X McCREERY
XX 5 POL
XXX II POL
XX 3 POL
XXXX 8 LEESE
XX 6

Polish advance, 17 May
Polish troops enter empty monastery, 18 May

Dora Line
Liri Valley
18 May
Gustav Line
Garigliano
Pignataro
Liri
San Giorgio a Liri
Sant Angelo
Sant Apollinare
Rocca
San Vittore del Lazio
San Pietro
XXX XIII
Mignano
Sant Ambrogio
XXX EXP JUIN
XXXX 5 CLARK

French advance over Aurunci Mountains, 13 May

Aurunci Mountains
Ausonia
Sant Andrea

Monte Cassino, 13–18 May 1944

GENERAL FRIDOLIN VON SENGER UND ETTERLIN (1891–1963)

The son of a German aristocratic family, von Senger und Etterlin joined the army in 1910 before going to Oxford University as a Rhodes Scholar. He served through the First World War and stayed on in the postwar army as commander of a cavalry regiment. He reached the rank of colonel by 1939 and fought in the Battle of France in command of his own mobile brigade. In October 1942, he commanded the 17th Panzer Division in southern Russia. As a lieutenant general he commanded German forces in Sicily in July and August 1943. On mainland Italy he commanded the 14th Panzer Corps and became a general of Panzer troops on 1 January 1944. He was opposed to Hitler but took no part in the assassination plot of July 1944. After the war he became a leading expert on German armoured forces and vehicles.

northeast while the French Expeditionary Corps made progress to the north. But on 11 February the first attack was called off, with total Allied casualties of 14,000, sustained in weeks of harsh weather and fierce fighting. A second assault was planned a week later using General Freyberg's New Zealand Corps, but Freyberg, anxious that German troops would use the monastery as a fortress, requested a preliminary bombing attack. Clark was unwilling, but he was overruled by Alexander, the Allied commander in Italy. On 15 February, 229 bombers pulverized the monastery into ruins.

It was only then that the German forces moved into the rubble, which provided good defensive positions. The only inhabitants of the monastery had been Italian civilians and a number of monks sheltering from the conflict, and between 300 and 400 were killed. On 15 February, the New Zealanders attacked the Cassino railway station while the 4th Indian Division attacked the monastery hill. After three days the offensive was called off after achieving almost nothing. Alexander then planned to wait until the spring to launch a more carefully prepared assault, but under pressure from London and Washington to give relief to the threatened Anzio beachhead, a third assault on Cassino was tried. After a massive air bombardment which turned Cassino into a ruin, the New Zealand Corps again tried to storm the town between 15 and 23 March, but after taking 4,000 casualties and battered by appalling weather, the attack was called off.

ABOVE A New Zealand anti-tank gun in action on 15 March 1944 during the attempt by the New Zealand Corps to seize the hill and monastery. After heavy casualties they were forced to withdraw.

BELOW Troops of the Polish 2nd Corps climbing the slopes of the monastery hill in May 1944. The Polish units took terrible casualties in the assault but fought with exceptional courage.

GENERAL WLADYSLAW ANDERS (1892–1970)

General Anders became famous in the Second World War as the leader of the Polish 2nd Corps which captured the monastery of Monte Cassino. The son of a German father, he was born in Russian-ruled Poland and fought in the tsar's army against the Germans during the First World War. After the war, he joined the army of the new Polish state as a cavalry commander. He was captured by the Red Army in September 1939 when Poland was invaded from the east, and imprisoned and tortured (though, unlike thousands of other Polish officers, not murdered). He was freed in July 1941 and then led a large force of Poles through Iran and Iraq where they met up with British forces and formed a Polish army corps. He fought in Italy and after the war stayed in Britain as a member of the Polish government-in-exile. He was buried in the cemetery at Monte Cassino among the soldiers he had led there.

The final assault was postponed until May. Alexander prepared a major operation, codenamed "Diadem", designed finally to unhinge the German line. The French forces in the south pushed across the Garigliano River and the Aurunci Mountains, threatening the whole south of the German line. The British 8th Army assaulted and finally captured Cassino, while on 17 May the Polish 2nd Corps under General Anders assaulted the monastery and after heavy hand-to-hand fighting, and losses of 3,500 men, occupied it on 18 May as German forces withdrew. The fourth Cassino battle persuaded Kesselring that his position was untenable and he began moving his forces back to the Gothic Line, north of Florence. Clark's 5th Army met up with Truscott's Anzio forces on 25 May. In the end, victory at Cassino was needed to rescue the Anzio operation, the opposite of what had been intended when the operations to break the Gustav Line were first launched late in 1943.

ABOVE Polish and British flags fly side by side above the monastery of Monte Cassino on 18 May 1944 after the German withdrawal. The capture of Monte Cassino paved the way for a rapid advance past Rome to Florence.

THE SECRET WAR: SPIES, CODES AND DECEPTION

The secret war of spying, deception code-making and code-breaking played an important part in the conduct of the Second World War for all the combatant powers. There were two main purposes behind the secret war: to shield from the enemy any knowledge of strategic and operational plans and force strengths, and to find out the plans and force strengths of the enemy. But there was also the possibility, exploited at times with remarkable success, of deceiving the enemy about operational intentions in order to maximize the chances of success and to get the enemy to dispose their forces at a disadvantage.

The most glamorous, but in many ways least successful, aspect of the secret war was spying. Most spies were caught if they operated in enemy country, and in many cases turned into double agents. In Britain a special double-cross organization, the XX-Committee, was set up under J C Masterman in September 1940 which succeeded in '"turning" a number of German spies and sending back misleading information to the German counter-intelligence organization, the Abwehr. Almost all German spies were caught, but so too were British agents in occupied Europe. The most successful spies were Soviet, but they spied on

ABOVE LEFT The US State Department official Alger Hiss was one of a number of high-ranking Soviet agents in the American administration. He was later accused by the House Un-American Activities Committee of working for Communism.

ABOVE RIGHT The chief of the German counter-intelligence organization (the Abwehr) was Admiral Wilhelm Canaris. He kept up the appearance of working enthusiastically for the regime but was in reality hostile to Hitler. After the July Plot in 1944 he was arrested and later hanged in April 1945.

their allies as well as their enemies. The Communist Red Orchestra spy ring was based in Göring's Air Ministry in Berlin until it was broken in 1942, but Soviet spies in Britain and the United States went undetected for years. The "Cambridge Five" worked at the heart of the British intelligence effort in MI6 and MI5, from where they fed a regular diet of information to their Soviet NKVD controller in London. In the Pacific War, the Allies made little use of spying, but Japanese spy networks in Hawaii and the United States supplied useful information before Pearl Harbor, though little thereafter.

Spying was a risky and unreliable source of information. During the war much more was expected from breaking enemy codes and ciphers. This was done routinely in most theatres, but the important point was to try to conceal from the enemy the fact that the codes had been broken. The Allies had a remarkable success in breaking German and Japanese codes and then preventing that knowledge from filtering back to the German and Japanese armed forces. The German Enigma coding machine, which was thought to be unbreakable, was first read in 1940, though very incompletely, but by the end of the war ULTRA traffic, as the British called it, could be read routinely and quickly. The effort to avoid giving any clue that the Allies could read their secret traffic was a major intelligence operation in its own right, but the Germans assumed that Enigma

BLETCHLEY PARK

Bletchley Park was a large Victorian country house northwest of London which became the home of the Government Code and Cypher School in 1939 under the codename Station X. It was the base for supplying secret codes and ciphers for use by British agencies but was also responsible for breaking enemy codes and ciphers. In 1942, it was renamed the Government Communications Headquarters. By 1945, around 10,000 people worked for the organization. It was famous for the work of Hut 6 where the German Enigma traffic was deciphered, and in June 1944 the first electronic computer, Colossus II, was introduced to help speed up the process.

RIGHT An inflatable dummy Sherman tank used in the deception Operation "Fortitude" to persuade the Germans that a large Allied army group was stationed in southeast England to attack the Pas-de-Calais in the summer of 1944.

was unbreakable and that the Allies got their information from other sources. The same was true in the Pacific where Japanese diplomatic traffic (PURPLE or MAGIC) and military traffic (ULTRA) was read by the Americans and the British, giving invaluable advance warning of Japanese moves after the disastrous failure at Pearl Harbor.

The third element of the secret war, deception, was perhaps the most important, because it could affect an entire campaign. The Allies had notable successes. The Soviet deception before the "Uranus" operation in November 1942 or Operation "Bagration" in summer 1944 was complete, and rapid victory in both cases owed a lot to the unpreparedness of Axis forces. The most famous was the "Fortitude" deception before D-Day, when an entirely fictitious army group (FUSAG) was set up in southeast England, with dummy tanks and bogus camps, to persuade Hitler that the assault would come across the narrowest part of the English Channel. A fake order-of-battle was also fed into German intelligence by double agents in Britain and the United States. So realistic was the deception that Hitler ordered large forces to remain in the Pas-de-Calais when they were desperately needed to repel the Normandy landings. British deception plans were carried out with particular skill and success, but this relied on the gullibility of the enemy. The German armed forces were less interested in playing deception games and so were an easy target for British ingenuity. The Allies in general made much greater use of intelligence as an arm of battle than did the Axis.

LEFT Four of the "Cambridge Five" who spied for the Soviets during the Second World War. Clockwise from top left: Anthony Blunt, Guy Burgess, Donald MacLean and Kim Philby. The fifth man, John Cairncross, was only exposed in the 1990s.

ABOVE General Heinz Guderian in his command vehicle watches soldiers sending messages using the Enigma machine. Some of the Enigma codes were regularly read by Allied intelligence from the early stages of the war.

MAJOR GENERAL WILLIAM J DONOVAN (1883–1959)

Donovan, always known as "Wild Bill" after his early student exploits on the American football field, was a successful New York lawyer, who served as commander of a volunteer regiment in the First World War during which he won three Purple Hearts and the Medal of Honor. He was a US attorney for Western New York, and during the 1930s became a confidant of President Roosevelt, who sent him to Britain as an emissary in 1940 and 1941 to assess British chances of survival. Here he met intelligence chiefs and began to argue for a co-ordinated American intelligence effort. In June 1941, Roosevelt named him co-ordinator of information to try to bring together the many departmental intelligence agencies under a single umbrella. In 1942, his organization was renamed the Office of Strategic Services, with Donovan in charge, responsible for intelligence and sabotage in Europe and Asia (except for the Philippines). The office was terminated in September 1945, but two years later the CIA was founded, modelled on Donovan's plan for a single peace-time intelligence department.

ENCLOSURES

1. A description of the imaginary agent 4 (3) created in order to channel misinformation to the Germans during Operation "Fortitude" in 1943–44, the deception plan for the planned invasion of France. The contact was identified by the double agent "Garbo" who played a key role in informing German intelligence about the fictitious First US Army Group (FUSAG) stationed in southeast England.

2. A diagram of the "Garbo" network of invented contacts which was used by double agent Jean Pujol, who worked for the British, to create the impression for German intelligence that there existed a real structure of informants and spies in Britain. His codename in Germany was Arabel.

OBJECT A nailbrush with a secret compartment carrying "escape aids" for SOE agents.

ABOVE The world's first computer was set up at the British code and cipher school at Bletchley Park to speed up the decrypting of the Enigma messages. Colossus II was in operation from June 1944.

BATTLE FOR INDIA: IMPHAL AND KOHIMA

11 MAY 1944
Alexander orders Operation "Diade", and the fourth battle for Monte Cassino.

4 JUNE 1944
US troops from Clark's 5th Army from the Anzio beachhead enter Rome.

6 JUNE 1944
Allied forces mount largest-ever amphibious operation against German-occupied Normandy.

13 JUNE 1944
First German V-weapon lands on British soil.

15 JUNE 1944
US air forces begin the bombardment of the Japanese homeland.

18 JULY 1944
General Tojo is removed as Japanese prime minister.

ABOVE Badge of the British 14th Army formed in November 1943 to defend India and Burma.

The Japanese in Burma intended to hold the country defensively to prevent the Allies opening a supply route from India to the Chinese forces fighting in southern China. But the incursion of Chindit units in spring 1943 persuaded the Japanese commanders that Burma might be made more secure by seizing a frontier zone around Imphal and Kohima in Indian Assam. Lieutenant General Renya Mutaguchi, appointed to command the Japanese 15th Army in Burma in March 1943, used his friendship with the Burma commander-in-chief, General Kawabe, to persuade the Tokyo government to endorse an attack on India, despite strong criticism of an operation in which supply would prove a permanent obstacle.

The Japanese plan for what they called Operation "U-Go" was to seize the main supply depot at Imphal, cut the road from the north at Kohima and then to dig in on the new frontier while monsoon rains prevented an Allied counter-offensive. As the operation was being prepared, British and Indian forces attacked Arakan in southern Burma and routed a Japanese force there, while in northern Burma General Stilwell, using Chinese forces assisted by the British Chindits and the American "Merrill's Marauders", launched a protracted campaign to try to seize the northern town of Myitkyina. Both operations effectively weakened the Japanese forces prepared for the Imphal-Kohima offensive, but it was possible to organize a total force of between 80,000 and 100,000 men for an operation which opened on 7 March with an attack by the Japanese 33rd Division from the south towards Imphal.

Despite intelligence warnings, the opening of a southern offensive surprised General Slim's 14th Army which made

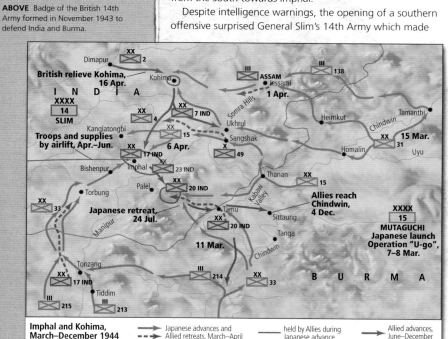

Imphal and Kohima, March–December 1944

→ Japanese advances and Allied retreats, March–April
--▶ held by Allies during Japanese advance
→ Allied advances, June–December

ABOVE Men of the West Yorkshire Regiment clear a Japanese roadblock on the road between Imphal and Kohima during the Japanese offensive in 1944.

GENERAL MASAKAZU KAWABE (1886–1965)

In March 1943, General Kawabe was made commander-in-chief of the Burma Area Army. A graduate of the army college in 1907, Kawabe was an infantry commander and in 1929–32 military attaché in Berlin. He was involved in the Marco Polo Bridge incident that sparked the Sino-Japanese war in July 1937, and became chief-of-staff of the Central China Expeditionary Army in 1938–39 and again in 1942–43. In Burma in 1944, he approved plans to invade India despite opposition from other senior commanders, but following their failure he was replaced and sent back to Japan in August that year. He joined the Supreme War Council, was promoted to full general and commanded first the Central Army District then the Air General Army (made up from all remaining aircraft in Japan) for the defence of the home islands. After helping to demobilize the army after surrender, he retired at the end of 1945.

ABOVE LEFT Japanese soldiers in the ruins of a building during Operation "U-Go" against Kohima and Imphal. The Japanese forces were poorly supplied and took heavy losses during the campaign.

BELOW A Japanese position under fire on the Tamu Road. British Empire forces had a considerable advantage in tanks and aircraft over the Japanese attackers.

a rapid retreat towards Imphal, leaving the Indian 20th Division stranded and surrounded around Shenam, where it held out against Japanese attacks. Slim airlifted two divisions from Arakan to reinforce the Imphal area and by the time Mutaguchi released the 15th Division towards the town, Slim had been able to organize the first stages of an effective defence. The Japanese force succeeded in cutting the roads to Imphal and there followed a four-month siege during which Slim was supplied by the RAF Third Tactical Air Force, bringing reinforcements, oil, food and military equipment.

Further to the north, Mutaguchi sent the 31st Division under Lieutenant General Kotoku Sato to seize Kohima and open up the possibility of capturing the more distant British supply depot at Dimapur. Struggling through mountainous jungle territory, Sato succeeded in bringing his whole division to Kohima, surrounding the town on 5 April and fighting street by street to capture it. By 18 April, the defenders were confined to one small hill but

a relief force sent down the road from Dimapur broke the siege and Sato found his forces pushed slowly back until, on 31 May, he ordered a general withdrawal of his exhausted and poorly supplied troops. The battle was hard fought, bringing 6,000 Japanese casualties but 4,000 British and Indian losses.

Mutaguchi's plan had been for Sato to seize Kohima and then send help south to reinforce the siege of Imphal. The failure further north left the Japanese facing a growing battle of attrition against a surrounded force too heavily armed to be decisively defeated. Slim's forces reopened the road from Imphal to Kohima on 22 June, breaking the siege, while the Japanese, short of food, ammunition and heavy equipment, and wracked with disease, fought an increasingly suicidal campaign. On 18 July, Kawabe and Mutaguchi agreed to terminate the operation and began a withdrawal that turned into a disastrous retreat as Slim's strengthened army pursued them across the Chindwin River. Japanese losses were 53,000, including at least 30,000 killed. The campaign broke the back of Japanese military strength in Burma and paved the way for the reconquest of the country in 1945.

BELOW Units of Slim's 14th Army open the road between Kohima and Imphal in June 1944, breaking the Japanese siege. Troops from Imphal met forces advancing from Kohima on the northern edge of the Manipur plain after ten weeks of heavy fighting.

ABOVE British soldiers search the long grass for Japanese snipers during the Battle of Imphal. They are covered by a Bren-gun unit in case of a sudden attack.

ABOVE RIGHT *Kukri* knives, a traditional Nepalese weapon used by the Gurkha divisions and also some Indian forces.

LEFT A Lee-Grant tank crosses a river north of the town of Imphal to meet the Japanese attack launched on 7 March 1944.

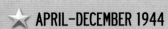

JAPAN'S WAR IN CHINA: OPERATION "ICHI-GO"

23 JUNE 1944
Start of the Soviet operation "Bagration" that destroys German Army Group Centre in a few weeks.

20 JULY 1944
Failed attempt by Colonel Claus von Stauffenberg to assassinate Hitler at his headquarters.

17 AUGUST 1944
Red Army units reach the German border in East Prussia.

25 AUGUST 1944
Paris is abandoned by the Germans after a week of fighting by the French resistance.

13 OCTOBER 1944
Red Army enters the Latvian capital Riga.

20 OCTOBER 1944
US 6th Army invades the island of Leyte in the Philippines.

11 NOVEMBER 1944
US Navy begins bombardment of Japanese island of Iwo Jima.

The military situation in China in the later stages of the war was one of great confusion. The Nationalists under Chiang Kaishek could see that Japan would be defeated and tried to conserve the strength of the Nationalist Kuomintang army for the expected postwar civil war with the Chinese Communists, who by 1944 had armed forces of around half a million men (and women), and a peasant militia estimated at two million. The Communists dominated parts of the northern countryside both inside and outside the Japanese area of occupation, but also avoided pitched campaigns against the Japanese. The most bellicose in China were the American commanders in the theatre, General Joseph Stilwell and the commander of the volunteer American air force, Major General Claire Chennault, whose "Flying Tigers" based in southern China organized the air supply of Chiang's forces over the "Hump" between India and China and flew missions against Japanese targets in occupied China.

It was the existence of the American air force bases in the southern provinces of Hunan and Guangxi, with the bombing threat they posed to the Japanese home islands, that prompted the Japanese commanders in China to undertake a renewed territorial offensive, the first since 1941. They also needed to open up a continuous rail link from Indo-China to Manchuria because the long sea routes had become dominated by American submarines and aircraft.

ABOVE President Roosevelt flanked by General Chiang Kaishek and his wife during a conference at Cairo in 1943. The Chinese leader hoped to get greater commitment from the United States for a campaign in Asia, but by the last years of the war it was evident that US forces could achieve Japan's defeat across the Pacific.

ABOVE Chinese workers in March 1944 build an airstrip with the help of American engineers. Here they can be seen taking stones to make the runways. The major US bases were overrun by Japanese forces during Operation "Ichi-Go".

Operation "Ichi-Go" (Number One) was launched in April 1944 when 150,000 Japanese troops seized the remainder of Henan province in central China and control of the Beijing–Hankou railway, meeting slight resistance.

The second phase began in late May 1944 with the drive to seize the southeastern provinces and eliminate Chennault's air bases. Stilwell warned Chiang and Chennault that unless adequate ground protection could be supplied by Chinese forces the air bases were not capable of defence. The Nationalist army numbered an estimated 3.5 million men, but many were loyal to local warlords and not reliable. Chiang organized a so-called Central Army of around 650,000 who were better armed and trained and loyal to him, but he was reluctant to commit them to pitched battle. The defence of the southeastern provinces

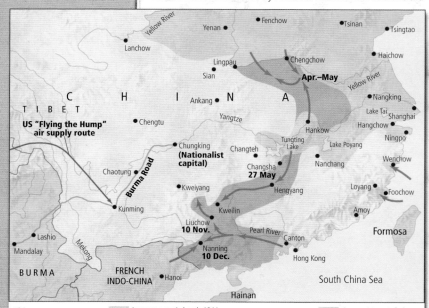

China, April–December 1944

- Japanese occupied, early 1944
- Japanese occupied after Operation "Ichi-Go", April–December 1944
- Communist controlled areas
- "Ichi-Go" advances

GENERAL JOSEPH STILWELL (1883–1946)

Stilwell was the leading American general in the Asian theatre of operations in China and Burma. He came from a strict Protestant background against which he was a natural rebel. Instead of Yale University he was sent to the Military Academy at West Point where he received demerits for laughing during drill. During the First World War he was intelligence officer for the US 4th Corps. In the interwar army his caustic style earned him the nickname "Vinegar Joe". He was military attaché to China, where he learned Chinese, from 1935 to 1939, and in 1942 he was selected to act as chief-of-staff to Chiang Kaishek and US commander-in-chief of the China-Burma-India theatre. In this role he found himself the victim of political intrigue and military rivalry and the corrupt exploitation of Lend-Lease supplies to China. In October 1944, after Chiang accused him of responsibility for failing to halt the Japanese "Ichi-Go" offensive, he was recalled to America, later serving as commander of the US 10th Army in Okinawa.

fell on the Cantonese forces of General Hsueh Yueh and Chennault's 200 aircraft. The city of Changsha, which had been defended by Nationalist forces earlier in the war, fell with little resistance on 18 June; then followed a drive by 350,000 troops through Hunan and Guangxi. Chinese resistance lasted six weeks but after that it crumbled and Chennault's air bases were overrun one by one. By November, Japanese troops had eliminated the last of them and linked up with forces coming from northern Indo-China to complete control of the rail link from Hanoi to Mukden in Manchuria. In the process Chinese forces suffered an estimated 500,000 dead or wounded.

"Ichi-Go" was then halted even though the road to the Nationalist capital at Chongqing, in central China, was now open and poorly defended. Japanese ambitions had been confined to establishing a rail route and destroying the American threat from the air. The Japanese army in China was not large enough to risk undertaking major expansion into the central regions. In much of the occupied area Japan relied on an estimated one million Chinese troops and policemen recruited from local Chinese puppet warlords or from bandits. Over the remaining nine months of war, Japan held on to its railway lines but control over the rural hinterland in the south was often nominal. The Nationalist army was better supplied in 1945 when the road from Burma was reopened, but the corruption and incompetence of the commanders and the uncertain loyalty of many of the troops prevented Chiang from playing any significant part in the final defeat of Japan.

MAO ZEDONG (1893–1976)

Mao Zedong was the leader of the Chinese Communists in the struggle against Japanese occupation and the Nationalist Chinese under Chiang Kaishek. The son of peasants, Mao became an active Communist in the 1920s, espousing a popular democratic ideology in contrast to the Stalinist outlook of European Communism. He helped to establish a rural Communist community in Jiangxi Province but was driven from it in 1934 by the Nationalist Army. There followed the Long March to Shaanxi province in the far north where a new Communist area was established around the city of Yenan. Mao emerged during the war as the dominant figure, leading a popular Chinese Red Army against the Japanese. By 1945, much of the northern countryside was under Communist control and four years later Communism triumphed in China. In 1949, Mao became chairman of the new People's Republic.

BELOW A Japanese prisoner captured by Chinese Nationalist soldiers during the Japanese campaign in Hunan province in central China in March 1944. Despite early Chinese resistance the whole area was captured by the Japanese army in summer 1944.

ABOVE A Chinese man tortured and murdered by Japanese forces after the fall of the city of Changsha on 18 June 1944. Roped to a wall, he has had both his eyes gouged out. Japanese forces exacted a terrible revenge on Chinese civilians throughout the occupied area.

ABOVE The skulls of 5,000 Chinese murdered by the Japanese in June 1944 have been laid out as a memorial to the dead on a hillside near the Chinese city of Hengyang in Hunan province.

INDEX

TRANSLATIONS

Page 11, enclosure 2 – Diary of Herbert Jesse

18 October: Us drivers kept digging on our own as the radio operators wasted time when collecting water and were deployed elsewhere by the drill sergeant.

19 October: Irmgard's birthday.
Kept digging, like yesterday. Boss was there and was amazed by the depth.

20 October: Lent the chief of staff 1000 C for [illegible].
Ordered "Battle of the DAK 41" for [illegible] C.

21 October: Drill, lessons, battle duties, which I had to perform since nobody else had a clue.
Guard duties as first sentry: 6p.m.–10p.m., 6a.m.–8a.m.

22 October: No guard duties in the morning.
Big command post exercise around lunchtime, but as reserve troop.

23 October: Sports, lessons.
8.45p.m. Tommi [British] commences raging artillery fire immediate alert on the whole front, got ready and drove to the Div. [Division]. Artillery fire continues, at night, too.

24 October: Visited by fighter bombers again. 5 km 10363. Constant bombings and attacks by fighter bombers. Tommi [British] made advances but was pushed back.

25 October: Frequent visits by bombers in the night. Vehicle dug in slightly. Quiet Sunday otherwise. 11p.m. Inroads by artillery, but no attack.

26 October: Frequent visits by bombers and fighters. Big wash in the afternoon. Cracked the first lice. Changed cover holes, since I was in the space of the 2nd Company.

27 October: Vehicle dug in. Took over guard duties. Air traffic busy. 2 Tommis [British] have been shot down.

28 October: Several bombing attacks again. Seconded to Panzer Pioneer Battalion 33 in the evening as Corporal Scheibe has had an engine failure. Drove up to III/IR105 with the pioneers and laid [illegible] before them. Very heavy artillery fire very nearby. 36 km 10399.

29 October: Back into the baggage room of the pioneers in the morning. Slept a little. Several

bomber attacks again. Heavy bombings at night, especially at the Ib. Quite a lot went up. 2 Tommis [British] crashed into each other.
30 October: Attacks by fighter bombers. Sandstorm. Intense radio traffic. Hellish artillery fire at night
31 October: Attacks by fighter bombers, heavy artillery fire.
1 November: Quieter than usual during the day. 2 kilo parcel with 2 [illegible]. Contents had turned into crumbs and 1 sausage, which tasted sensational. Tommi [British] invaded on a large scale during the night.
2 November: Various parts are retreating. Heavy artillery fire, but the pioneers are staying. Towards the evening the Battalion retreats in the former command post of the Div.
3 November: Seconded to Pz.Jger 33 [tank destroyers] in the morning. To Lieutenant Zahn who has been decorated with the Ritterkreuz. Seconded to Panzer Battalion 605 in the afternoon, to Captain Fischer, beyond the telegraph road. Heavy artillery fire all day long. At night the front recedes. Constantly got stuck in the sand and lost unit.
4 November: Drove around on my own at night. 30 km 10429. Arrived at the 164th Div early in the day. There I drove back to the front with a liaison officer. Unit under heavy defensive fighting. Heavy artillery fire. General retreat via Bir el Tamar in the evening. Only brief rest at night. 46 km 10475.
5 November: Onwards, back to Elevation 146, 19km SSW Railway kilometre 220. Brief stop here. The onwards on my way back. Returned to the Div. at night. Reserve radio post. Zahn onwards towards West-North-West to 20km South-South-West of Mersa Matruh. 187 km 10662.
6 November: Engine failure in the morning. Succeeded in getting it afloat at the last second and looked for Div. Finally found it. Slept a little. Collected provisions. Very heavy showers in the morning. Seconded to Pz.Jger 33 [tank destroyers]. 6 km 10668.
7 November: Finally able to sleep at night once again, as I was able to switch off. Worked on the engine and mechanics [Maschinensatz] with I troop. Marched onwards in the evening. Fierce fighting with our own Sperrverband, as the agreed signal flares were not set off. Losses: 2 tanks, 2 dead, 6 wounded. Then marched onwards. Along the Siwa Road.
8 November: Brief stop in the morning. Then onwards on the Via via Sidi el Berani, stopping 39 km past it. Up until now I have constantly been driving on my own and have acted as troop leader. I'm at the end of my rope. Just happy that it is still working out. Buqbuq.
On both days: 183 km 10851
9 November: In the morning we advance along the sea at the head of the Div. Crossed the Halfaya Pass at 2.40p.m., onwards via Musaid to Elevation 206, South-South-West Capuzzo. Into position here. 71 km 10922
10 November: MY BIRTHDAY
Heavy bombings during the night. Quiet in the morning, collected provisions for the long run (26 loafs of bread for 4). Quiet day. Talked to Leo Freund about university studies.
11 November: Marching onwards to the Capuzzo Trigh at 3am in the night. Stopping at elevation 213. Engine damage again. The gasket at the head in the upper part of the fuel pump. Found it myself, even though a battalion saddler sergeant major [Oberschirrmeister] was looking for it for half an hour. But I was completely on my own there. Onwards up the Trigh until just before El Adem. 109 km 11031.
12 November: 5am onwards through El Adem. Stopped South of it and into position. 5pm onwards on the Via d'el Aore and on the Acroma Road westbound. In the night by two gentlemen [fell behind [illegible]] without me noticing it. Then back to the Div. 78 km 11109.
13 November: Saw the boss early on: am to be punished with 5 days of intensified as I supposedly neglected my duties. Several dressings-down all day. I'm sick of it. Again the officer is [illegible]. Stopped by Temrad in the evening. 51 km 11160.
14 November: 4am Marching onwards on the Martuba Road to Maraua. Stopped where the tracks cross: Mechili-Derna Road and Martuba Road. Onwards on the bypass around Derna, then to Maraua on the Via Balbia. 245 km 11405.

Page 19, enclosure 1 – Soviet Aerial Propaganda leaflet dropped on Germam troops.

General Field Marshal Paulus
On captivity under the Russians
German Officers and Men!

Hitler has finally lost the war – this is a fact that nobody can change and nobody can deny.

German generals, officers, NCOs and privates are becoming increasingly convinced that: any further sacrifice is futile, particularly as they will not change the balance of forces on the fronts;

Because the war is being fought on German soil, Hitler is not only sending men to a futile death, but also destroying their homes, robbing them of their last crust and turning them into beggars;

It is better under such circumstances to surrender, spend a few months as a Russian prisoner of war, and thereby to save your life and to care for your family again after the war.

In January and February this year alone, 350,000 German men, officers and generals surrendered to the Red Army. Over 80 distinguished German generals, tens of thousands of German officers and over one million German men are already prisoners of war with the Russians.

What are their lives like in Russian captivity?

General Field Marshal Paulus, who capitulated with the rest of the German Sixth Army at Stalingrad in 1943, provides a clear answer:

"It is a sordid lie if Mr Himmler claims that German soldiers are treated inhumanely in Russian captivity, and that they are forced to make propaganda against their own country with whips and shots to the back of the head.

The truth is rather that German prisoners of war in the Soviet Union are treated humanely and properly."

(from the General Field Marshal Paulus' appeal "To the German people" of 26.10.44)

Other prominent German generals in Russian captivity can vouch for the same.

Page 19, enclosure 2 – Proclamation issued by Hitler to German troops at Stalingrad, 26 November 1942.

Soldiers of the Sixth Army and the Fourth Panzer Army!

The battle for Stalingrad is reaching its peak.

The enemy has broken through in the rear of the German troops and is now vainly attempting to bring this important stronghold on the Volga back into his possession.

My thoughts and the thoughts of the entire German nation are with you in these hours of hardship!

You must at all costs hold on to the position of Stalingrad, which was won with so much bloodshed under the leadership of your energetic generals!

You must be unswerving in your resolve, as in Kharkov in spring, to ensure that the Russians will be annihilated by this breakthrough.

I shall do everything in my power to support you in your heroic circles.

Adolf Hitler

Page 19, enclosure 3 – Summary of the operations at Stalingrad, drafted by Stalin and broadcast to the nation.

RESULTS OF THE RED ARMY OFFENSIVE FROM 10 NOVEMBER 1942 TO 31 MARCH 1943

On 31 March this year, the Red Army completed its winter advance against the German fascist troops.

The offensive of the Soviet troops, which continued for 4 months and 20 days (**and was completed as a result of a great**) is the greatest in the history of modern warfare, both in the scale of military action, and as regards the military strategic results obtained.

During their advance, Soviet troops inflicted severe military defeats on the enemy army.

As a result of battles lasting several days at the approaches to Vladikzvkaz, in mid November 1942 our troops struck a blow on the group of German fascist troops routing a number of enemy units and ending the threat hanging over the Soviet Caucasus and its oilfields.

On 19 November 1942 our troops located on the approaches to Stalingrad went on the offensive and surrounded the German fascist troops, who numbered at least 330,000 men and officers. The historic battle of Stalingrad ended on 2 February 1943 with the total victory of the Red Army and a defeat of the German fascist troops unprecedented in the history of warfare.

On 25 November Soviet troops went on to the offensive in the areas east of the town of Velikie Luki and west of the town of Rzhev. Our units advanced significantly, taking the most important enemy railway communication lines [hand-writing illegible], ~~destroying more than 75,000 German men and officers, and capturing a huge amount of materiel.~~

On 16 December the Red Army struck a new blow against the enemy in the Middle Don region. In just a fortnight our troops advanced 150-200 kilometres, defeating 15 enemy divisions and capturing ~~60,050 enemy men and officers~~ a large amount of materiel and taking many prisoners.

On 22 December our troops in the south went on a decisive offensive, breaking down enemy resistance, and in battles lasting several days cleared the Northern Caucasus and Kuban of German fascist troops.

In the area south of Stalingrad in battles lasting from 12 to 30 December, our troops defeated a an enemy strike force attempting to break through to the German fascist troops surrounded by the Red Army at Stalingrad.

On 13 January Red Army units south of Voronezh advanced, breaking through strong enemy defences in three directions, destroying and capturing several enemy divisions, and liberating hundreds of towns and villages

After seven days' fierce fighting, the troops on the Leningrad and Volkhov fronts, overcoming a long-established enemy defence lines up to 14 kilometres deep, broke through to the river Neva, joining up on 18 January and thereby breaking the blockade of Leningrad.

On 27 January our troops located west of Voronezh advanced, surrounded and destroyed a large concentration of German fascist troops in the region east of Kostornoye. In its advance on this section, the Red Army liberated hundreds of centres of population, including the city of Kursk.

On 1 March, the Soviet troops completed the liquidation of the fortified enemy bridgehead in the region of Demyansk. In 8 days of fighting our units liberated 302 centres of population, including the city of Demyansk.

In early March, after a decisive offensive in the Central Section of the front, Soviet troops **broke through heavily defended lines of the German front** and took the cities of Rzhev, Olenya, Sychevka, Bely and Vyazma, thereby eliminating the bridgehead which the enemy had relied upon to strike at Moscow.

In 4 months and 20 days the Soviet Army, in extremely difficult winter conditions, advanced westwards **as far as 600**- 700 km in some sectors. Soviet troops liberated a vast area of 480,000 square kilometres from the enemy, ~~whose Soviet population in 1939 had been as much as 20 million~~. As a result of the Red Army's advance, regions of major economic and military strategic importance were liberated from the enemy. The oblasts of Voronezh and Stalingrad and the autonomous republics of Checheno-Ingushetia, Northern Ossetia, Kabardin-Balkharsk and Kalmykia, the Stavropol kray, the Cherkes, Karachayevsk and Adygeya autonomous regions, almost the entire kray of Krasnodar, the oblasts of Rostov and Kursk were liberated in their entirety, and a significant part of the Smolensk and Orlov oblasts including dozens of major cities and many thousands of villages were liberated from the German invaders.

In repelling the enemy westwards, the Red Army liberated major waterways and railways of the country, including the Volga road which was re-instated after being broken by the enemy in Autumn 1942, and cleared the entire course of the river Don of enemy troops. The following main railway lines were liberated from enemy hands and put into operation: Stalingrad-Povorino, Stalingrad-Likhaya- Voroshilvgrad, Stalingrad-Krasnodar, Vladikavkaz-Rostov-on-Don, Liski-Millerovo Shakhty – Rostov-on-Don, Elets-Kostornaya-Voroshilovgrad, Moscow-Vyazma, Moscow-Rzhev-Velikie Luki, and many others.

During the Red Army advance from 10 November 1942 to 31 March 1943 our troops captured the following trophies: **[1,490]** aircraft, **4,670** tanks, **15,360** cannon of various calibre, ~~32,400~~ machine guns, ~~9,900~~ mortars, ~~4,934~~ anti-tank guns, ~~80,640~~ sub-machine guns, ~~449,000~~ rifles, ~~around 17,000,000~~ shells, ~~128,500,000~~ bullets, ~~1,542~~ radio transmitters, ~~123,000~~ vehicles, ~~18,000~~ motorcycles, ~~1,460 tractor units and carriers, 30,000 horses, 32,720 carts, 890 locomotives, 20,000 carriages, 1,825 warehouses of various types,~~ and many other types of military equipment.

During that period 343,525 enemy men and officers were taken prisoner.

From 10 November 1942 to 31 March 1943 our troops destroyed 3,600 enemy aircraft, 4,520 tanks, 4,500 guns, 3,900 mortars, 10,100 machine guns and 22,500 sub-machine-guns **5,090 aircraft, 9,190 tanks, 20,360 cannon**

[blue ink:] all [illegible] **during our winter** [illegible]

During the same period the enemy lost more than 850,000 men and officers killed in action.

The losses of Soviet troops from 10 November 1942 to 31 March 1943 were: men dead or missing, aircraft, tanks, cannon of various calibre.

The advance of the Red Army in winter 1942-1943 showed that the course of the war between Hitler's Germany and the Soviet Union had been turned by the Chiefs of Staff of the Red Army, the military actions of our troops and its allies were now to the benefit of the Soviet Union and the detriment of Germany and her vassals. Our troops' successes undermined enemy morale, sowing uncertainty and doubt in victory in his ranks. The Red Army has conducted a single campaign offensive against the united armed forces of Germany, ~~Austria~~, Italy, Finland, Hungary, Romania and Slovakia and inflicted severe losses ~~and securing a breakthrough in the course of the war.~~ The enemy has now been repulsed to the regions it occupied in the battles of summer and autumn 1941. In 4 months and 20 days of fierce fighting, the Red Army has liberated from the German swine territories which it took the enemy more than one year and several million [...] men and officers to conquer. It is therefore clear that our troops have learned to beat the Germans, and gained experience in major offensive battles, ~~[...] the expulsion of the Germans from the territory of our country and established the conditions needed for successfully fighting the enemy in decisive battles to come.~~

However, the Soviet people and the Red Army **are aware that the enemy is not beaten yet, and the battle with [...]** should not rest on their laurels. The enemy is making desperate attempts to scrape together new troop contingents through his renowned "total mobilisation". The Hitlerite scum are an underhand, low and treacherous enemy. They are capable of any foul deeds only to succeed. We are still faced by a long [...], bloody battle to free our country from the German fascist bandits. We must mobilise our whole potential and strength to further and to build on the successes achieved by the Red Army in the winter of 1942-1943, and to achieve a decisive victory over the enemy.

SOVINFORMBURO

Page 25, enclosure 1 – Italian safe conduct pass

YOU CAN NO LONGER ESCAPE THE JAWS OF THE VICE!
SAFE CONDUCT

This leaflet is to be considered as a Safe Conduct: the prisoner bearing it is entitled to the treatment proper to Prisoners of War and to the valiant opponent who answered this appeal to Italian soldiers to prevent needless bloodshed.

Italian soldiers!

Yesterday In El Alemain, the Germans stole your means of transport and you went on foot
Today You have fewer vehicles, less fuel, less lubricant.
Tomorrow Your "Allies" will be driving in cars and you will be on foot.
Pawns in a German war for German interests, you will be forced to retreat first to Tripoli and then to Tunis, 1000 kilometres backwards.
1000 Km ON FOOT
WHILE THE GERMANS ARE DRIVING YOUR OWN VEHICLES
1000 kilometres on foot to end up in the allied trap in Tunis!

Page 37, enclosure 1 – German proclamation on acts of resistance

Proclamation to the French population

Anti-German radio propaganda and agents in the pay of the Allies have called upon you to stage strikes, insubordination and sabotage against transport and supply installations.

Under the pretext of doing so to strike at the German occupying forces, you are being called upon to carry out acts whose consequences will affect yourselves, your wives, your children, threatening your supplies and your security.

The German occupying authorities are resolved to re-establish respect for the laws and ordinances issued and to re-establish order and social peace and will if necessary do so by force of arms.

I therefore order that: Every working person must immediately continue their work and thereby contribute to public order. In this way they will serve the interests of their country and their family.

Anyone who stops work or refuses to return to work, who shuts out workers or prevents those wishing to work from starting work again, harasses them, threatens them or otherwise disturbs the peace, is in breach of Article 20 of the Ordinance on the Protection of the Occupying Authorities and will face severe penalties, including death.

To re-establish peace and order, I hereby order that:

1.All places of entertainment, theatres, cinemas, etc, be closed until further notice.

2.The sale of alcohol and alcoholic drinks is forbidden.

3.Gatherings on streets and squares and any assembly in enclosed areas other than by families and by workers carrying out their work is forbidden.

People of France, I appeal to you for sense! Anybody who fails to comply with my orders will face the full force of the law and the use of weapons by the troops.

Der Militärbefehlshaber in Frankreich

Page 49, enclosure – Partisan Order

Tomorrow I Strictly secret I Order I 5 September 1942 I No. 00189 I Moscow

Contents: The tasks of the partisan movement

For a second year now the Soviet Union is conducting its great patriotic war against the German fascist hordes, which treacherously raided the territory of our country.

After subjugating and plundering the whole of Europe, the German imperialists have now turned their sights on putting the peoples of the Soviet Union under German subjugation. The enemy has succeeded in taking Ukraine, Belarus, Lithuania, Latvia, Estonia, Moldova and part of the Northern Caucasus, and is continuing to blockade Leningrad. Undeterred by his vast losses, the enemy is throwing all his forces at the front line and is continuing to force his way deep into our country.

At this time of gravest peril for all the peoples of the Soviet Union, every citizen, man and woman, in the front line and in the rear, on the occupied territories and in partisan units, face one single task, and that is to defend the motherland, to uphold freedom, independence, their honour, and to rout the odious German invaders.

The Red Army is heroically rebuffing the onslaught of the enemy and dealing him crippling blows. It is harassing his forces and inflicting heavy losses on him.

The workers of the Soviet Union in plants and factories, at collective farms and cooperative farms, are working selflessly to produce arms, munitions, equipment and provisions for the Red Army. Our industry is now working to meet the needs of the front line. The army is now taking delivery of sufficient tanks, aircraft, artillery, mortars and ammunition. The military might of the Red Army has grown significantly, and continues to do so.

But the German armies can only be defeated the by joint action of the Red Army on the front line, and forceful, constant blows by partisan units in the enemy's rear.

The history of warfare teaches us that invaders are often beaten not just by the struggles of a regular army, but also by popular partisan movements which help in the final overthrow of the invaders.

This was the case during the patriotic war of 1812. Napoleon, who was trying to conquer our land, was finally defeated by the Russian army, supported by an armed populace which carried on a merciless partisan struggle in the enemy's rear. The Napoleonic Army, at that time the most powerful in the world, left its bones in Russia because alongside the regular Russian Army, a popular partisan movement rose in defence of the motherland.

It was the same in the years of civil war. The Red Army defeated the army of the interventionists on all fronts, and defended the fledgling Soviet Republic, which was in mortal danger, thanks to the armed struggle of the entire people and an organised partisan movement in the rear of the enemy army.

Now with the Red Army's forces struggling on the front line to defend the freedom and independence of its state, the people's partisan movement on the territory of our country temporarily occupied by the German occupiers is becoming a decisive condition for achieving victory over the enemy.

The Germans may have captured our territory, but have not succeeded in subjugating the Soviet people. Our people loathe the occupiers, they are taking to arms and organizing a partisan struggle in the German army's rear. The partisans are inflicting serious damage on enemy troops, men and materiel, and sowing confusion in the enemy's rear. However, the partisan movement has not yet reached its full potential, it has not yet become the cause and each and every one who find themselves in the enemy's clutches, as all conditions are now at hand for the rapid development of an all-people's partisan movement against the German occupiers.

The partisan movement must above all develop more broadly and with greater intensity; it has to incorporate broader masses of the Soviet people in the occupied territories. The partisan movement has to become an all-people's movement.

This means that existing partisan units should not close their ranks, but draw in broader sections of the population into the partisan struggle. Along with the organization of many partisan units, trusted partisan reserves must be established among the populace to replenish existing partisan units, or to set up new ones. Things must be organized so that there is not a single town, village or centre of population on the territory under temporary occupation without clandestine fighting reserves for the partisan movement. These clandestine fighting reserves must not be limited in number, but include all upright citizens all men and women who want to free themselves from the German [aggressors].

The fundamental goals of the partisan movement are: destroy the enemy's rear, destroy his [illegible] and other military institutions, destroy his railway and bridges, [illegible] and [illegible] and barracks, destroy the enemy's men, capture or destroy representatives of the enemy's authorities. Destroying the supply routes of the enemy is now of the utmost importance. The enemy now needs to throw reserves, materiel, fuel and munitions at the front from deep in the rear, and also transport [illegible], bread, meat, [and materiel] plundered in our country to Germany. The railways and roads the enemy needs to supply his forces now stretch over thousands of kilometres. These pass through forests in many places, providing favourable conditions for the operation of partisan groups in destroying supply routes. Cutting supply lines means depriving the enemy of his capacity to deliver personnel, materiel, fuel and ammunition to the Soviet Union, and also to take back to Germany the material assets plundered from our country, and thus supporting the Soviet Union in defeating the enemy.

The implementation of these fundamental tasks requires that all partisan groups conduct broad-scale partisan combat operations, as well as sabotage, terrorist and espionage operations in the rear of the enemy.

I HEREBY COMMAND:

1. For the purposes of disrupting rail traffic, and undermining regular transport operations in the enemy's rear, the use of all means to cause railway accidents, to blast railway bridges, to blow up or burn down station facilities, to blow up or fire station equipment, to blow up, burn and fire at locomotives, trucks, tank trucks and railway sidings. The destruction of any personnel, materiel, fuel, ammunition and other goods, along with any locomotives and trucks as survive. The destruction of road bridges and viaducts, rear rallies and other man-made installations. Corralling his horses. Rendering installations, transports and goods unusable by all possible means where use cannot be made of them.

2. The destruction of military garrisons, headquarters and institutions, military units, men and officers acting alone, and guards stationed on transports and at warehouses.

3. The destruction of warehouses and dumps of arms, munitions, fuel, provisions and other materiel, garages and repair workshops.

4. The destruction of railways, roads and tracks, the annihilation of radio communications equipment, the cutting and removal of cables, the cutting down and burning of telegraph posts, the destruction of radio transmitters and operating personnel.

5. Attacks enemy aerodromes and aircraft, hangars, fuels and ammunition dumps, annihilation of aircrews and maintenance staff and guards.

6. The destruction of all economic command posts, enemy foragers, food requisitioning teams and agents, attacks on stores of plundered food, silos and grain elevators; distribution of the bread to the populace wherever possible, and where not, its total destruction.

7. Partisan attacks have not yet reached the cities. Partisan units, individual organisations and saboteurs must penetrate all large and small towns, and carry on extensive espionage and sabotage there. They must destroy and set on fire centres of communications, power stations, boiler plants, water supplies, warehouses, fuel depots and other targets of military and economic importance.

8. The relentless elimination or capture of fascist political figures, generals, high-ranking officials and traitors of all ilk who are in the service of the enemy. To this end, the maintenance of constant surveillance of all generals and high-ranking officials, the establishment of what they do, where they live, where and when they work, where and how they travel, whom they know among the local population, how they behave, who is guarding them and how.

9. Constant espionage by partisan units and individual fighters to assist the Red Army:

a) by specially selecting persons capable of conducting underground espionage and their infiltration into the local government and administration set up by the Germans, into factories, depots, stations, post offices, telegraph and telephone exchanges, aerodromes, warehouses and stores, as bodyguards for high-ranking Germans, into the Gestapo and its schools, and in all other institutions and agencies serving the army or the local German administration.

b) by constant surveillance of troop locations and movements, railways and roads, ascertaining troop numbers and types, the identifications of units, the quantity and nature of military equipment, movements and travel times; establishment of watch procedures and the strength of military squadrons and transports;

c) by establishing the precise locations of troops and staffs, their names and numbers, the institutions and bodies of the occupying authorities;

d) by gathering intelligence on enemy aerodromes, the number and types of aircraft permanently or temporarily based at particular aerodromes, on aerodrome installations, auxiliary and special vehicles, on stocks of fuel and oil, and on ground-based and air-based aerodrome defences.

e) by organising espionage in towns and major centres of population in order to establish troop number in garrisons (numbers of types of troops, name, identifications and commands of units); anti-aircraft defences; military stores and workshops; the military industry; higher military and civil administration;

f) by establishing where defence lines have been built, their type, how they have been technically equipped, their armaments and communications equipment, and whether they have garrisons;

g) by tracking and precisely recording the results of bombing raids by our air force;

h) by using all means possible to intercept orders, reports, operational charts and other enemy documentation.

Data intercepted by agents and partisan field units must be immediately forwarded to the headquarters of the partisan movement.

10. That the central bodies of the partisan movement, commanders and commissars of partisan units, in addition to military actions, draw up and carry on constant political work among the populace, explaining the truth about the Soviet Union, about the merciless struggle of the Red Army, and the entire Soviet people against the fascist invader, and the inevitable demise of the bloodthirsty occupiers. That they expose the lies of German propaganda by facts, and imbue a feeling of hatred and rancour towards the German invaders. To this end, newspapers, leaflets and other printed matter should be distributed in the occupied territories.

The Supreme Military Command of the Red Army requires that all leading bodies, commanders, political agitators and fighters in the partisan movement conduct an even broader and more intensive struggle in the enemy's rear without giving him any respite. This will be the best and most valuable support they can provide for the Red Army.

Through combined action by the Red Army and the partisan movement, the enemy will be destroyed.

People's Commissar for Defence
I. Stalin
To be sent to all chiefs of staff, partisan units, the members of military [illegible] of fronts and armies.

CREDITS

The publishers would like to thank the following people for thier valuable assistance with the preparation of this book:

Imperial War Museum: Department of Documents: Tony Richards, Rod Suddaby, Simon Offord, Stephen Walton; Department of Exhibits and Firearms: Alan Jeffreys, Paul Cornish, Fergus Read; Department of Art: Pauline Allwright; Department of Printed books: Christopher Hunt, Jane Rosen and all those in the Reading Room; Photograph Archive: Richard Bayford, Glyn Biesty, Damon Cleary, Richard Ash, Yvonne Oliver; Sound Archive: Margaret Brooks; Department of Exhibitions: Andrew McDonnell, Laurence Burley, Stephen Clark; Public Services: Terry Charman, Abigail Ratcliffe, Madeleine James

The National Archives, Kew: Paul Johnson, Hugh Alexander
Churchill Archives Centre, Churchill College, Cambridge: Allen Packwood, Caroline Herbert
Service historique de la Défense, Château de Vincennes, Armée, Paris, France: Bertrand Fonck
Sergei Kudryashov
Gina McNeely
Barbara Levy

PHOTOGRAPHS

The vast majority of photographs reproduced in this book have been taken from the collections of the Photograph Archive at the Imperial War Museum. The museum's reference numbers for each of the photographs is indicated below, giving the page on which they appear in the book and location indicator.

Key: t = top, b = bottom, l = left, r = right and c = centre.

Imperial War Museum: 7tc (E 8487), 7tr (E 15223), 7bl (TR 2283), 10cl (E 18474), 11tr (E 18971), 11cr (E 21333), 11tc (E 18980), 12cl (A 12661), 12bc (A 12649), 12tc (TR 285), 20tc (NY 6082), 21br (K 5870), 22tr (SE 7946), 22br (HU 6643), 22cr (MH 7877), 22br (SE 7910), 23bc (SE 7921), 23tr (IND 2290) 23br (HU 6643), 25br (NA 2876), 26cl (C 3717), 26bl (HU 92132), 27tl (CH 11047), 27cl (CH 18005), 27bc (HU 4594), 27r sequence top to bottom (FLM 2339), (FLM 2340), (FLM 2342), 28tr (D 8463), 28cr (PST 8105), 29bl (D 2894), 29tr (PST 696), 32cl (CAN 902), 32tr (A 17916), 32cr (EA 38785), 32br (NA 4940), 33tl (NA 5854), 33bl (A 18492), 33r (NYF 9892), 34cr (C 3677), 35tl (CL 3400), 35r (BU 5077), 36tl (ZZZ 11837E), 40tl (A 19246), 40c (NA 6157), 40tr (NA 6630), 41tr (CNA 1700), 41bc (NA 142), 41br (NAM 57), 44br (NYF 11281), 46bl (E 26634), 46br (TR 153), 47tl (A 20731), 47tr (A 20744), 48bl (MISC 60756), 49tr (PST 3075), 50tr (A 20687), 50br (ART LD 7424), 51b (A 21200), 51tr (A 22633), 51c (A 16489), 52tr (AI 13229), 52c (IA 19828), 52bl (NA 11041), 52br (NA 12136), 53br (NA 15295), 53tc (NA 15306), 54cr (MH 6352), 54tc (MH 11250), 55br (MH 1680), 55bl (MH 1978), 55tc (NA 12810), 56bc (H 42531), 58br (IND 3331), 58bc (IND 3430), 59cl (IND 3468), 59tl (IND 3479), back endpaper (AI 13229)

Photographs from sources outside the Imperial War Museum, with the kind permission of the following:

AKG-Images: 9bl, 16c, 16tr, 17cl, 18c, 18br, 19br, 21tr, 25c, 26tr, 27c, 30tr, 31bc, 36br, 38tr, 39c, 39tr, 51tc, 58tc, 60c; /RIA Novosti: 8tr, 9tr, 38bl, 48tc; /Ullstein Bild: 30cl, 31tl; **/Alinari:** 10tc, 11bl; **/Australia War Memorial:** 42br (016422), 42tr (042999), 42r (127965), 42c (REL34921), 43bl (070242), 43br (042740), 43tr (P00554_002); **/Cody Images:** 36bc, 39r; / **Corbis:** 19tl, 20cl, 24br, 31tc, 33tr, 34bl, 44l, 44tr, 45br; /Bettmann: 16br, 19bl, 20br, 21cl, 21tl, 29br, 29tc, 34tr, 45tl, 48c, 53c; 58tr, 60tr, 61bl; /The Dmitri Baltermants Collection: 17tr, 18tc; /Hulton-Deutsch Collection: 12tr, 47br; **/Getty Images:** front endpaper, 8bc, 9tl, 13tr, 14c, 15r, 17bc, 25tl, 28bl, 31cr, 39bl, 45cl, 46tr, 47bl, 48br, 51bc, 56cl, 56bl; /AFP: 37tr; / National Geographic: 18bl; /Popperfoto: 8tl, 55tr; /Time & Life Pictures 6tc, 17tc, 23tl, 45l, 45bl, 49c; **/The Granger Collection:** 28cl; **/Library of Congress, Washington:** 53bl, 57tr; / **Mary Evans Picture Library:** 6br; **/PA Photos:** AP Photo: 14tl, 14br, 15cl, 15tl, 38br, 61br; / DPA: 37b; **/Photos12.com:** Coll-DITE-USIS: 13tl, 37cr; /Oasis: 36tr; **/Private Collection:** 14bl, 50bl; **/Rex Features:** Snap: 20bl; /Scala Archives: 8cl, 31tr, 34br, 35cl, 57tc; **/Topfoto.co.uk:** 11br, 13br, 25bl, 30bc, 41c, 43cr, 49br, 57bl, 59bl, 61cr; /RIA Novosti: 49cl; **/Roger-Viollet:** 53tr; /Ullstein Bild: 9tc, 10bc, 13c, 19cl, 24tr, 24bc, 28br, 41bl, 54br

Every effort has been made to acknowledge correctly and contact the source and/or copyright holder of each picture, and Carlton Books apologizes for any unintentional errors or omissions, which will be corrected in future editions of this book.

OBJECTS
Imperial War Museum
Text in brackets indicates Imperial War Museum reference numbers.

6 (INS 8038), 9 (OMD 9562),10t (INS 5110), 10b (INS 5132), 12 (FLA 5494), 16 (OMD 9560), 18 (INS 7807), 23 (INS 7092), 24 (INS 5326), 32 (INS 5154), 34 (FEQ 0866), 36l (EPH 4313), 36r (INS 8078), 38l (OMD 9563), 38r (FIR 6123), 40 (INS 5262), 42 (AWM PEL 34921), 48 (INS 8053), 52l (INS 5463), 52r (MUN 3314), 57 (EPH 8486), 58 (INS 4079), 59 (EPH 0187)

FACSIMILE MEMORABILIA
With the kind permission of:

Imperial War Museum
Text in brackets indicate Imperial War Museum reference numbers or departments.

11 enclosure 1 (Documents), enclosure 2 (Documents); **19** enclosure 1 (K85/3770), enclosure 2 (816 XX02 (Spec Misc B6); **23** enclosure 1 (K44654); **25** enclosure 1 (K82-1752); **37** enclosure 1 (IWM PST 4106); **53** (1437 87/23/1)

Imperial War Museum and:
Papers of the Rt Hon Viscount Montgomery of Alamein CMG CBE: **11** enclosure 3 (Documents); **25** enclosure 2 (Documents)
Papers of Sergeant K R Wyse: **23** enclosure 2 (12714 03/33/1). With kind permission of Mrs Hilary J Wright.

Memorabilia from sources outside the Imperial War Museum:
Text in brackets indicate archive reference numbers.

The National Archives of the United States of America: **13**; **25** enclosure 3; **33** enclosures 1 and 2; **45** enclosures 1,2 and 3

The Archive of Journals Rodina and Istochnik: **19** enclosure 3; **49**

The National Archives, Kew: **37** enclosure 2 (HS6-595); **57** enclosure 1 (KV2–41), enclosure 2 (KV2–41)

Every effort has been made to acknowledge correctly and contact the source and/or copyright holder of each piece of memorabilia, and Carlton Books apologizes for any unintentional errors or omissions, which will be corrected in future editions of this book.

PUBLISHING CREDITS

Editorial Director: Piers Murray Hill

Executive Editor: Gemma Maclagan

Additional Editorial work: Philip Parker

Design Director: Russell Porter

Art Director: Russell Knowles

Design: Russell Knowles

Cartography: Martin Brown

Picture Research: Steve Behan

Production: Lisa Cook